JOHN REDMOND

POSTAGE

REVENUE

1

1

ONE PENNY

REDMONDUS REX.

(*Design for the Irish Penny Postage Stamp.*)

'Remondus Rex'

Historical Association of Ireland
Life and Times Series, No. 8

John Redmond

PAUL BEW

Published for the
HISTORICAL ASSOCIATION OF IRELAND
By Dundalgan Press Ltd

First published 1996
ISBN 0-85221-130-9

© Paul Bew 1996
Cover design: Jarlath Hayes
Cover illustration: Chandler Collection
Frontispiece: 'Redmondus Rex' in *Punch*, 1 May 1912
Historical Association of Ireland, Dublin
Printed by Dundalgan Press, Dundalk

FOREWORD

This series of short biographical studies published by the Historical Association of Ireland is designed to place the lives of leading historical figures against the background of new research on the problems and conditions of their times. These studies should be particularly helpful to students preparing for Leaving Certificate, G.C.E. Advanced Level and undergraduate history examinations, while also appealing to the general public.

CIARAN BRADY
EUGENE J. DOYLE
Historical Association of Ireland

PREFACE

This life of Redmond, short though it is, owes much to the stimulation and support of others who work in the field of modern Irish history. In particular I am grateful to my friend and frequent co-author, Henry Patterson. Robert Kee suggested in the *T.L.S.* that I should write a biography of Redmond. Roy Foster's interest in Redmond's 'sense of all-Irelandism, his hard-headed bourgeois virtues, his Castle Catholic self-confidence, his realisation of the advantages to be had in co-operation with Britain' also helped to make the project attractive. It is anyway hard to resist an Irish nationalist politician who could be described by a party colleague, Serjeant Sullivan, as being 'slow, cautious, cynical with a prejudice in favour of truth that was almost English'. Two volumes already published in the same series by close colleagues are devoted to Redmond's contemporaries—they are Alvin Jackson's *Sir Edward Carson* and Patrick Maume's *D. P. Moran*. They provided a model and a challenge. Dr Maume's broad scholarship in this period influenced my approach at many points. Mrs Máiréad Maume also kindly provided a valuable reference. Above all, Greta Jones sustained me with her wry understanding of the significance of Redmondism in Irish history.

PAUL BEW
Department of Politics
Queen's University of Belfast

CONTENTS

CHRONOLOGY   1

INTRODUCTION   3

1. Emergence of a Parnellite   6

2. 'Parnellism' without Parnell   18

3. Chairman of the Party   24

4. An Imperial Nationalism?   32

5. After the Easter Rising   40

CONCLUSION   48

NOTES   52

SELECT BIBLIOGRAPHY   58

CHRONOLOGY OF REDMOND'S LIFE AND TIMES

1856   Born at Ballytrent, County Wexford, son of William Archer Redmond, Home Rule M.P., and his wife, Mary, daughter of Major Hoey of Hoeyfield, County Wicklow.

1868–74   Educated at Clongowes College.

1874   Enters Trinity College, but leaves in 1875 without a degree.

1876   Decides to live with his father in London with a view to becoming a barrister; acts as his father's assistant at Westminster.

1877   The Redmond brothers are taken by their father to attend the London hotel reception for the release of Fenian prisoner, Michael Davitt—their first recorded political act.

1879   Davitt founds the Land League with C. S. Parnell, M.P. for Wicklow, as President.

1880   Nominated for a clerkship in the House of Commons. Openly commits himself to Parnell, the rising star, and the Land League, the rising force of Irish politics. William Archer Redmond dies.

1881   Enters House of Commons as Nationalist member for New Ross; a strong supporter of Parnell and the Land League movement.

1883   With his brother Willie arrives in Adelaide, Australia, on fund-raising mission for the Parnellite party. Both brothers marry into the prosperous Daltons, an Irish-Australian family.

1886   Gladstone introduces the first Home Rule Bill.

1888   Imprisoned for five weeks on a charge of intimidation in an agrarian case.   .

1889   Redmond's wife dies; there were three children from the marriage.

1890   The 'Parnell split' resulting from the O'Shea divorce crisis; Redmond and his brother side with the Parnellite minority.

1891   Following the death of Parnell, Redmond, now the leader of 'Parnellism', resigns Wexford, his seat since the Redistribution Act of 1885, and stands unsuccessfully for Cork, which Parnell had represented; he does, however, win a seat in Waterford a few months later.

1893   Gladstone introduces the second Home Rule Bill; Redmond's speech establishes him for the first time as a major House of Commons figure.

1895   Redmond supports moderate Unionist Horace Plunkett's Recess Committee, which leads to the establishment of the Department of Agriculture and Technical Instruction in 1899.

1899   Marries his second wife, Ada Beesley, an English Protestant; they have no children.

1900   Elected chairman of the newly united Irish Parliamentary Party.

1903   Wyndham Land Act; Redmond is forced to tone down his early enthusiasm for this act because of a more jaundiced attitude on the part of those close to John Dillon in the Irish Party.

1906   Liberal landslide victory in general election ends almost twenty years of Conservative electoral hegemony.

1907   The Irish Party convention, at Redmond's bidding, firmly rejects government's devolution proposals; some believe that Redmond had initially been rather more sympathetic.

1909   Birrell Land Act; like the Wyndham Act, this leads to further serious division of opinion among Nationalist M.P.s.

1910   The two general elections of 1910 at first give, and then confirm, Redmond's possession of the balance of power in the House of Commons.

1912   Apparently a year of triumph. The third Home Rule Bill introduced by the government with every hope of passing into law—but the real difficulty lies in Ulster; there Unionist opinion mobilises in the most militant fashion.

1914   Redmond and Unionist leader Edward Carson fail to shape a compromise at the Buckingham Palace Conference of 21–24 July. A few days later the First World War breaks out; Redmond commits Ireland to support of the British war effort.

1915   Coalition government formed in London; Redmond is offered, but refuses, a place in the cabinet; Carson, however, accepts a similar offer and joins the cabinet as Attorney-General.

1916   Easter Rising launched by radical separatists in Dublin; Redmond has no sympathy for the rebel leaders.

1917   Willie Redmond dies gallantly at the front; in July his seat in East Clare is won by Eamon de Valera, symbolising the shift of support away from the Irish Parliamentary Party and towards those associated with the Easter Rising. Redmond makes one last unsuccessful effort at the Irish Convention to reach a compromise with the forces of Irish Unionism.

1918   Following an operation in March, Redmond at first makes good progress, but then suffers heart failure and dies a few hours later on 6 March.

INTRODUCTION

In his brilliant book, which draws both on the skills of the scholar and the insights of the practising politician, Stephen Gwynn described the striking but bitter paradox of John Redmond's career:

> No man holds power forever, and during seventeen continuous years he held the leadership among his own people with far more than all the personal ascendancy of a Prime Minister in one of the overseas dominions: and held it without any of the binding forces which control of administration and patronage bestow. He left his people improved in their material circumstances to an almost incredible degree, as compared with their state when he began his work. Yet Ireland counts his life as a failure and he most assuredly accepted that view.[1]

From the turbulent epoch of the Land League crisis of 1879–82 until his death in 1918, John Redmond was at the centre of Irish political affairs and thus of Anglo-Irish relations. In this period the agrarian revolution initiated by the Land League transformed Irish life. The landlord system in Ireland went into decline, while peasant proprietorship blossomed. Other major reforms were achieved, most notably in the field of Catholic education. Redmond was very proud of the scope of these social reforms, but throughout most of his career he suffered from the inevitable comparisons which were drawn between himself and the charismatic Charles Stewart Parnell, the Home Rule leader of the 1880s. Parnell brought the cause of Irish self-government, which was languishing in the 1870s, to the verge of success in 1886. Redmond, by contrast, appeared to be unable to surpass this level of achievement, even though he inherited a movement of much greater substance.

One of Redmond's contemporaries, Michael MacDonagh, the author of a fine study of the Home Rule movement, expressed this idea with some clarity:

> Parnell excelled in daunting a hostile House of Commons. The role of Redmond was that of retaining and increasing the confidence of a friendly House—a humbler, but still a

3

valuable qualification for leadership in altered times.
Unluckily, in the process of winning England, Redmond lost
Ireland, and he lost it, his enemies said, for want of that
swiftness of decision and iron purpose by which Parnell
impressed himself on the imagination of his countrymen and
on the fears of their oppressors.[2]

As Francis Cruise O'Brien noted in 1910, the negative
comparison of Redmond with the more glamorous Parnell had
become a 'commonplace' of political commentary. As O'Brien
also pointed out, it was hardly a fair comparison. Parnell had a
'young party' at his disposal while Redmond led a 'middle-aged'
party. Perhaps even more important, he added, 'in Parnell's day
the struggle was literally one of life and death, and felt as such; in
Mr Redmond's day, the struggle, is not literally one of life and
death, or at all events, is not appreciated as such'.[3] These are
valid points. O'Brien offered a ringing defence of John Redmond
against his critics: 'Time will bring them all to its reckoning, and
Mr Redmond's name will be the one name left. History is always
revenged on the crowd.'[4] But this argument was based on an
explicit assumption—'Some day Mr Redmond will be the Prime
Minister of Ireland'—which was to be proved, all too painfully,
false. As one of Redmond's last letters—to a close friend, Michael
Governey of Carlow—explicitly acknowledged, 'history' is not
always 'revenged on the crowd'. Outlining the failure of his own
project, Redmond foresaw only 'universal anarchy . . . when every
blackguard who wants to commit an outrage will simply call
himself a Sinn Féiner and thereby get the sympathy of the
unthinking crowd'. In an eerie echo of Francis Cruise O'Brien's
turn of phrase, he sadly acknowledged: 'The strong man today, I
am sorry to say, in Ireland is the man who shouts with the biggest
crowd.'[5]

Even so, it is surprising, indeed, that the present short work is
the first biography of Redmond to appear since Denis Gwynn's
The Life of John Redmond, which came out in 1932. The years since
the start of the Ulster troubles in 1968 have seen many biogra-
phies devoted to men who were Redmond's contemporaries and
yet were rather shadowy figures as far as the great bulk of the Irish
public were concerned—men like Pearse, Connolly or Casement.
The reason is not hard to find: the participation of Pearse,
Connolly and Casement in the Easter Rising of 1916, which led to

the foundation of the independent Irish state, has seemed to validate their lives. At the same time, it appeared to invalidate Redmond's political principles, which are perceived to be those of a weak-kneed and ineffectual constitutionalism; this is certainly how Redmond is viewed by extreme nationalist journals like *An Phoblacht* or the *Sunday Business Post* and even by some writers in the *Irish Times*.[6] Yet matters are perhaps more complex. At a time when 'exclusively democratic methods' and 'purely peaceful means' are being urged with renewed vigour in Ireland it is surely appropriate that Redmond's career, which was devoted to these principles, should be reconsidered.

Redmond was much denounced in his lifetime by radical nationalists for his failure to stop Irish emigration or to bring about Irish political unity. It has to be said that his critics—many of whom were to wield governmental power in an independent Ireland—can hardly claim in their turn to have been successful in these respects. The *Irish Times* claimed in a recent editorial, provoked by an attack on the 'Redmondite instincts' of the Taoiseach, Mr John Bruton, by the leader of Fianna Fáil, Mr Bertie Ahern: 'If a solution [to the Ulster crisis] emerges through the initiatives now in hand, it will be precisely because of the triumph of Redmond-like virtues—compromise, tolerance, negotiation and a commitment to the democratic process.'[7] Such a claim will not be accepted by everyone—but it does serve to illustrate the importance of Redmond's legacy in Irish political life.

This little volume cannot replace the need for a new full-scale biography of John Redmond. Peter Leppard is working on such a project under the supervision of Professor Roy Foster of Hertford College, Oxford. But it can raise some of the issues about Redmond which have for too long been suppressed in modern Irish historical debate.

1

EMERGENCE OF A PARNELLITE

John Edward Redmond was born on 1 September 1856 at Ballytrent House, an old family mansion on the coast of Wexford overlooking and facing the Tuskar lighthouse. He was the product of a Catholic gentry family which had overcome loss of land in the seventeenth century by emerging as successful merchant traders in the late eighteenth and nineteenth centuries. This local conception of the Redmond family as 'good old stock' was an invaluable political asset throughout his career.

Yet Redmond's immediate background was rather more complex. Redmond's uncle, General John Patrick Redmond, who inherited the family estate, had been awarded a C.B. for his role during the Indian mutiny. His father, William Archer Redmond (educated at Stonyhurst and Trinity College, Dublin) was a Home Rule M.P. for Wexford, who generally supported the moderate views of Isaac Butt, the founder of the Home Rule movement in 1870. William Archer Redmond did, however, take his two sons to the reception in a London hotel in 1877 for the release of the celebrated Fenian prisoner, Michael Davitt; this seems to have been the first political meeting the two young men had attended. On the other hand, Redmond's mother, Mary Hoey, came from a Protestant and Unionist background. While it is true that she later converted to Catholicism, she certainly never converted to nationalism. In general, the marriage seems to have been a slightly distant one. All of this meant that the political inheritance of the Redmond brothers contained no simple or automatic message, nor indeed did the immediate history of the county in which they were raised. The involvement of County Wexford in the rising of the United Irishmen in 1798 was of special significance. John Redmond himself was certainly not one who feared to speak of '98:

> My boyish ears had listened to the tales of '98 from the lips of
> old men who had themselves witnessed the struggle, and I

6

scarcely knew a family who can not tell of a father or grand-
father or some near relative who died fighting at Wexford or
Oulart or Ross. Every scene most familiar to my early youth
was associated with some tale of heroism or suffering, and
one of my proudest recollections has ever been, as it is today,
that in that dark hour of trial there were not wanting men of
my race and name who attested by their lives their devotion
for Ireland.[1]

It all depends, of course, on how devotion to Ireland is assessed.
At the height of Redmond's political fame and success, the
nationalist press carried a rather fetching portrait of a 'Miss
Redmond' riding to the aid of the rebels; indeed, a maternal
ancestor, William Kearney, had been hanged in 1798—but
another paternal ancestor, William Redmond, had been on the
side of the yeomanry.[2] John Dillon, Redmond's nationalist parliamentary colleague, always believed that the Redmond family in
the 1790s were prosperous drapers who were more conservative
than their Protestant neighbours. Ancestral voices, therefore, did
not utter any clear or unambiguous message.

From 1868 to 1874 Redmond was educated at the Jesuit college,
Clongowes Wood (where his brother William later attended).
Clongowes then was the principal school for the Irish Catholic
middle class; it did not have a nationalist reputation. Both John
and William frequently expressed their intense affection in later
years for their *alma mater*. John was regarded as the best speaker
of the college debating society, and when plays were produced by
the dramatic society, he usually took the leading part. After
leaving Clongowes, Redmond—and this was then a rather
unusual step for a Catholic to take—entered Trinity College,
Dublin; as one of his biographers puts it, Trinity was seen as 'a
stronghold of the Protestant mind in Ireland'. But as the same
writer also notes, 'John Redmond never said a bitter word of
Trinity, and it was there indeed that he learned to appreciate the
qualities of Protestant Ireland.' According to his biographer
Warre B. Wells, 'From the first he contemplated Anglo-Saxon
civilisation with a sentiment akin to awe.'[3] But W. M. Crooks, an
English friend of Redmond's from this time, put it more accurate-
ly when he referred to 'the touch of cosmopolitanism'[4] which was
always present in Redmond's intellectual make-up; Redmond was
incapable of that visceral hostility to the broader culture of the

United Kingdom which so animated a radical nationalist ideologue like Arthur Griffith.[5]

From Trinity College, John Redmond proceeded, without completing a degree, to King's Inn, Dublin. He intended to follow the profession of a barrister; but although he was eventually called to the Irish bar in 1887, Redmond was always more interested in politics. In 1876 he moved on again and went to London to help his father in the House of Commons, taking up a position, which his father had obtained for him, as a salaried clerk at £300 per annum in the vote office.

In the later 1870s he watched closely as Charles Stewart Parnell, a Wicklow squire, made himself the focus of a semi-revolutionary coalition: while remaining a constitutionalist, Parnell made a definite appeal to neo-Fenians, who, in turn, mobilised the peasantry, especially in the west, in an often violent struggle against landlords. The young John Redmond—setting aside perhaps a certain natural conservatism—was highly impressed by the style and effectiveness of the new leader. In the spring of 1880 Redmond supported Parnell at a meeting in Enniscorthy when supporters of the then representative of County Wexford, Keyes O'Clery, attacked Parnell's platform. Sticks were freely used, and Parnell himself was almost dragged by the legs off the platform. Redmond was knocked down by the crowd and his face cut. 'Well,' said Parnell drily, 'you have shed your blood for me at all events.' Nevertheless, Parnell was not over-impressed by the young Redmond's claims; when William Archer Redmond died later in 1880, John Redmond naturally sought Parnell's support as the natural successor to his father as M.P. for Wexford. Parnell, however, insisted that his then secretary, Tim Healy, was the better candidate. Redmond reluctantly swallowed his disappointment; early in the next year he was to become the official candidate for New Ross, then a parliamentary borough, and was returned unopposed. Tim Healy claimed—with what authority it is not clear—that at this point Willie Redmond sent John a telegram saying: 'For Gods sake don't disgrace the family by joining the Land League and Parnell.'[6] Even if this is true, within six months Willie was a mainstay on League platforms; more immediately, John rushed straight away to the House of Commons, which was in the midst of a stormy session as the Nationalist M.P.s protested against the arrest of Land League leader, Michael Davitt. Redmond reached the House, but could not yet participate in the debate, as he had not been sworn in as a member; he could only watch as the Speaker suspended all the Irish members who were taking part in the debate. The next day the newly elected member for New Ross took his seat, and it was his unique experience, as he himself used to recall afterwards, 'to take his seat, make his maiden speech and be expelled by force from the House of Commons all on the same evening'.[7]

Throughout 1881 Wexford was a loyal Parnellite county—sometimes impressively so. As the climax of the Land League crisis was reached, Parnell chose to deliver his final rhetorical defiance of Gladstone—'a masquerading knight-errant, this pretended champion of the liberties of every other nation except those of the Irish nation'—at the 'greatest demonstration ever witnessed in Wexford' on 9 October. According to Parnell, there was 'no moral force behind English rule in Ireland'. Gladstone, however, felt differently: the Prime Minister genuinely believed that the Tyrone by-election of September 1881 had shown a majority of even the local Catholic electorate to be in favour of his brand of Liberal reformism and against the Land League candidate.[8] On 13 October the government had Parnell arrested, and subsequently the Land League was suppressed. Wexford remained loyal to Parnell, sometimes excessively so; for Parnell, as he wrote to Mrs O'Shea at the moment of his arrest, was relieved that the movement was 'breaking fast'.[9] Although areas of the county such as New Ross and Ramsgrange had spontaneously thrown up tenants' defence organisations to take the League's place, Wexford accepted Parnell's prison *diktat* that these bodies be abandoned even though they had been advocated by 'true and able friends of the popular cause'.[10] The Wexford hounds were stopped hunting on 2 December by a large crowd of farmers and labourers who shouted that they would not allow hunting until Parnell was released. (Ironically, Parnell had renewed his personal subscription to the Wicklow Harriers the day before his arrest.) But in the main Wexford's participation in the land war had been a relatively moderate one. Certainly Redmond had few of the embarrassments arising out of violence and assassination which so marked parts of the west of the country. No doubt this was in part because, as William Redmond explicitly stated, 'landlordism' had traditionally been a softer, milder regime in Wexford in comparison with other parts of the country. Unlike the vast majority of young Parnellite lieutenants, including his brother Willie, John Redmond was able to stay out of jail. By pure good luck (as Tim Healy pointed out), Redmond won the ballot for the right to sponsor a land bill in early 1882 in the House of Commons, and this bill became the focus of attempts to forge an accommodation between Gladstone and Parnell.

This was perhaps just as well, because John Redmond did not make a very convincing revolutionary. It was not just his personal reserve combined with marked fastidiousness which made him visibly uneasy in the presence of less well-groomed members of the public; it was a deeper question of political temperament. As one of his early biographers, Warre B. Wells, noted with some insight,

> Like Parnell, Mr Redmond scarcely shared the social revolutionary spirit which inspired much of the agitation of the Land League. It is not to say that he did not recognise and feel for the misery of the small Irish tenant farmer, or that he did not desire the establishment of a peasant proprietary, with, to that extent, the downfall of the landlords in Ireland. But he was not in his element in what took on, in effect, the character of a social revolution. He was not a democratic leveller like Davitt. Had Ireland been a self-governing country in the early 80s, and Mr Redmond Prime Minister, we may be sure that he would have proposed a reform of the land system; equally sure, however, that he would have discouraged, taken action against, many of the methods adopted by the agrarian agitators . . . When men like Parnell and Redmond identified themselves with radical enterprises like the Land League it was partly for the purpose of maintaining a national unity of means and ends, and partly because such enterprises served to intimidate British statesmen and made Ireland difficult for them to govern, thus improving the prospects of home rule.[11]

But, as Wells was aware, there was another aspect to this problem: a latent class loyalty on the part of both Parnell and Redmond. As Wells pointed out, Harold Spender, the Liberal commentator, could see this clearly enough. Spender wrote in the *Contemporary Review* for April 1918: 'Like all landlords [Redmond] could not put entirely aside the clan feeling for his class. There he was the follower of Parnell. Right through the heart of the nationalist fight, Parnell was always held back by a strain of sympathy for the landlords.' But, as in Parnell's case, there were many landlords—including close family connections— who could not see Redmond's residual conservatism. As Stephen Gwynn noted in his *D.N.B.* entry with some insight, 'The political struggle, then virtually a class war, estranged him from his own class and even from his kin. His childless uncle [General John Patrick Redmond] so arranged his will that the inheritance was financially and politically a burden.'

In January 1883 John and Willie Redmond travelled to Australia to raise funds for the Irish Parliamentary Party and the National League. John had been selected for the task because of his reputation for moderation, (Thomas Brennan, one of the most revolutionary Land Leaguers, had wanted the job). Even so, the Redmonds had a difficult time; they were pursued by the bad publicity resulting from the Phoenix Park murders trial. Even Sir Bryan O'Loghlen, a family friend of the Redmonds, declined to give them public sponsorship. Redmond later recalled that the success of his work was entirely due to Irish-Australian working men. By the end of 1883 £15,000 had been sent back to Ireland to pay the expenses of the party—money raised mainly by lower middle-class and working-class Irish-Australians. But one rather wealthy Irish-Australian family, the Daltons, did give full support to the Redmonds. The Redmond brothers responded 'in a unique and unarguable fashion'—they both married into the Dalton family. In September 1883 John Redmond married the Dalton brothers' half-sister Johanna in Northern Sydney. Later Willie married James Dalton's daughter Eleanor. In a rather strange incident, however, Thomas Curran and James O'Connor—both loyal political allies—made it aggressively clear to John, on the day before his wedding, that they viewed him as a mere adventurer who had come to Australia to get himself a wife and a fortune.[12]

Politically, the Redmonds were relatively well attuned to Australian mores. Although John was always resolute, he avoided extremism; Lord Loftus, the Governor of New South Wales, reported to the Colonial Office, that his later lectures in particular were lucid and moderate. When the Redmonds moved on to America, their tone had to change. 'While they were in Australia, the danger was to avoid being too disloyal: in America the danger was to avoid being too loyal!' In America Redmond certainly struck a more militant note: on one occasion in August 1886 he told an audience in Chicago:

> We are working not simply for the removal of grievances . . . The principle embodied in the Irish movement is just the same principle which was the soul of every Irish movement for the last seven centuries—the principle of rebellion against the rule of strangers; the principle which Owen Roe O'Neill vindicated at Benburb, which animated Tone and Fitzgerald, and to which Emmet sacrificed a blameless life.[13]

While absent in Australia, Willie Redmond won a by-election victory over the O'Conor Don, the Liberal candidate in Wexford. The O'Conor Don was, the nationalists admitted, an excellent candidate—'with some of the glamour of the son of an Irish king around him'[14]—and the result was therefore all the more significant: 'Whiggery was buried in Wexford'. Even in his absence, though, Willie Redmond was able to play on the family name. Tim Healy illustrated the point with a forceful anecdote: 'One of his [the O'Conor Don's] supporters said to an illiterate voter, "You had better mind where you will get your bread if you vote for Redmond" (*groans*) and he then said to him "I got my bread from the Redmonds before I broke a crust of yours."'[15] This was a tribute to the role played by the Redmond family in the development of Wexford. On one level, the victory of Redmond over the O'Conor Don was a victory for popular democracy over elitism; but, as this anecdote shows, looked at more closely it was a victory for the more tactically populist wing of the Irish Catholic elite.

In the great set-piece debates of 1886 which followed Gladstone's dramatic concession to Home Rule, Redmond played a relatively insignificant role. But he did articulate one proposition which illustrated the 'liberal imperialism' which was the great intellectual legacy of his Australian visit.

On the question of retaining Irish members at Westminster after Home Rule, Redmond declared: 'As a Nationalist I do not regard as entirely palatable the idea that forever and a day

Ireland's voice should be excluded from the councils of an empire which the genius and valour of her sons have done so much to build up and of which she is to remain.'[16]   He was, of course, touching on one of the great constitutional difficulties posed by any scheme of devolution and going rather against the grain.   On 8 April 1886 Gladstone argued that it was impossible, after Home Rule, to allow Irish members to come back to Westminster even for 'imperial concerns', because these were impossible to distinguish from other business of the House.[17]   By July 1888, however, Gladstone had adopted Redmond's position: 'It [the retention of Irish members] is a matter on which I never had the slightest intention or disposition to interpose an objection.'[18]

Following Gladstone's failure to secure the passage of the Home Rule Bill, the Conservatives returned to power.   Redmond seems to have shared the Irish Party consensus that the Conservatives should not be allowed to govern by the use of the ordinary law.   He offered his own analysis at Glenbrien, County Wexford:

> Mr Gladstone, on the contrary, told the people of England that they had to choose between 'coercion' on the one side and Home Rule on the other.   Home Rule was defeated at the last election in Great Britain and I say advisedly that if in the face of that defeat the Tories had been able to rule Ireland with the ordinary law, the result would have been, in England and Scotland, to throw back their cause, perhaps for a genera-tion and to give the lie direct to the prophecy of Mr Gladstone . . . We have been able to force the government to give up the ordinary law and to fall back once more on Coercion.[19]

This calculation, rather than any deep-rooted agrarian radicalism, explains Redmond's commitment to the renewal of rural militancy known as the Plan of Campaign launched at this juncture by William O'Brien—with very little backing from an increasingly conservative Parnell.   It was a commitment which was in the end to land Redmond in jail for the first and only time in his life.   In 1888 he was charged with using the language of intimi-dation against a landlord, Colonel Walker, in a speech at Scarawalsh.   Colonel Walker's eviction of a tenant was the subject of this speech: the facts of this case were so unjust, alleged

Redmond, that no tenant would take the farm and Walker would have arrayed against him the united hostility of the entire people of his locality. At his trial Redmond took on his own defence and argued in vain that he had used the language of prophecy, not intimidation. Unsurprisingly, it was not a successful defence; on the other hand, by the standard of the 1880s, Redmond's platform rhetoric at Scarawalsh was in no way remarkable. He was sentenced to five weeks' imprisonment with hard labour. He was treated as a common criminal, not as a political offender. He had to wear prison clothes; he was deprived of pen, ink and paper; he had no book to read except the Bible. For a time he was even put on a diet of bread and water because he refused to walk round the exercise yard in the company of the 'rogues' and 'vagabonds' of the neighbourhood.[20]

Nevertheless, although his prison sentence was a useful badge of honour, Redmond was not in the top echelon of Irish Party M.P.s. He was, however, undoubtedly becoming a prominent figure 'in the second eleven' by the end of the 1880s. At this moment the general trend in politics was for the Liberal–Nationalist alliance to become stronger; on 18 December 1889 Parnell and Gladstone enjoyed very positive discussions at Hawarden on the possible shape of the Home Rule settlement.[21] Then, on 24 December 1889, Captain William O'Shea, a former Irish M.P., filed a petition for divorce from his wife, citing Parnell as the co-respondent. In that same month Redmond was, however, hit by a deeper personal tragedy. Redmond and Johanna Dalton had had two daughters and a son; then in December 1889 Johanna, who had apparently been in 'good health and spirits',[22] died suddenly when Redmond was away from home on political duty. Until his death Redmond kept, among other personal relics of his family, a lock of his wife's hair and the little wild flower which she had given him the first day they met.[23] Ten years later Redmond was to marry again; his marriage to Miss Ada Beesley—an English Protestant—of Leamington, Warwickshire, brought him 'much domestic happiness and unfailing devotion'.[24] Ada shared completely Redmond's 'fastidious dislike for the intrusion of public curiosity upon his private life'.

But in 1890 Redmond was lonely and to some extent adrift; the world of politics provided no relief. In November 1890 it was announced that Parnell would not oppose the divorce petition. Redmond was in Clonmel, attending a court case arising out of the Plan of Campaign. He immediately told a journalist friend: 'I don't know what you will do, but I will stick to Parnell.'[25] In the event, a majority of Parnell's party felt rather differently. Within the party meeting Redmond emerged as the principal defender of 'the master of the party', but Tim Healy's savage quip 'Who is to be the mistress of the party?'[26] carried the day. Redmond, at last, and only at this point, had, however, now won Parnell's respect. As Francis Cruise O'Brien recalled,

> In the bitter day of harsh and unforgiving words in Committee Room 15, amidst all that scene of upbraiding and the unfolding of terrible consequences, one hears the note of affection and tenderness from the lips of Parnell. The proud and scornful eyes soften for just an instant; 'My friend, Jack Redmond' he says . . .[27]

For the first time Redmond was acknowledged as an intimate friend; it was perhaps worth some of the generalised anguish of the split.

But the going was to get tougher. By-elections were lost by the Parnellites, and on 25 June 1891 Parnell married Katharine O'Shea at the Steyning registry office. A Tory and Unionist peer, Lord George Hamilton, responded sympathetically: 'I have always felt that although he was no doubt morally guilty of an infraction of the Decalogue by his relations with Mrs O'Shea, his extraordinary affection for her, the protection which he gave her, and the utter subordination of everything political to what was for her benefit show that there was an element of great tenderness in his character.'[28] But it was a shocking moment for mainstream Catholic Ireland. A close ally and kinsman of Tim Healy, Alexander Sullivan, wrote: 'Katharine O'Shea had been a partner in a Catholic marriage—to go through the ceremony of marriage with one who claimed to be liberated from the bond of a Catholic union was an insult to the Catholic Church.'[29] There can be little doubt that Redmond's instinctive reaction was closer to the view of Alexander Sullivan than to that of Lord George Hamilton. After all, Redmond's 'general view of life was that of the Irish country gentlemen. He was a traditionalist in religion.'[30] Redmond's public identification with Parnell diminished

somewhat. It was alleged that he was about to break with
Parnell—certainly he was advertised to speak at Parnell's final
meetings at Listowel, Westport and Creggs, but did not do so.
Nevertheless, there was to be no public break with the 'chief'.

There was undoubtedly a social dimension to the loyalty of the
Redmond brothers. Grouse-shooting was one of Redmond's
favourite sports. This created a connection with Parnell, who
often paid more attention to his beautiful red setter, Grouse, than
to his colleagues at party meetings and dinners. As Alexander
Sullivan noted, 'Parnell was more than a bit of a snob. He was
always conscious of the vulgarity of the Party standard, as
compared with the culture of his own class.'[31]   But he did have
close relations with those Irish Party M.P.s (the Redmond
brothers, William Corbett and Dick Power) who were 'country
gentlemen' and who shared his tastes in country life, his love of
sport, his 'affection for a setter'. Redmond's speech when the
party fell apart in bitterness in Committee Room 15 in December
1890 also shows that he feared that the sacrifice of Parnell meant
the loss of independence of the Irish Party and its absorption into
Gladstonian Liberalism. It may be that after his wife's death
Redmond's natural emotional conservatism was beginning to
reassert himself and that he responded to the growing conservatism of Parnell's own thinking, especially on agrarian matters.[32]
When Parnell's premature death came on 6 October 1891,
Redmond was now the only plausible leader of the Parnellite
cause. On a more personal level, his name was now to be linked
with the Parnell family in a peculiarly intimate way.

In the confused state of Parnell's finances after his death,
Aughavanagh, his shooting lodge in County Wicklow, had to be
disposed of. Some friends of Redmond decided later that for his
'services to Ireland' he should receive the title-deeds of
Aughavanagh. This cost the subscribers £250 between them. T. P.
O'Connor recalled wryly: 'In Redmond's time it was the symbol of
contradictoriness and the down-at-heelness of many Irish things,
especially in the landlord class that even in my own youth was still
the omnipotent factor of Irish life. It stood on a hill, many miles
from everybody and everything; it consisted of a centre which was
fairly comfortable, but on both sides there was a gaping wound
where the wall stood bare and empty with no roof upon it.'[33]

Terence de Vere White has written: 'The history of the two men [Parnell and Redmond] and of their respective families illustrates perfectly the contrast between the Anglo-Irish and the older stock.'[34]   But through their common possession of that half-ruined shooting-lodge, Aughavanagh, they are linked and associated in the mind's eye in a rather melancholy image.[35]

2

'PARNELLISM' WITHOUT PARNELL

On the morning of Parnell's funeral in October 1891 John Redmond was elected chairman of the remnant of the Irish Party which adhered to the Parnellite cause. Redmond decided to resign his seat and to stand for the constituency of Cork City left vacant by Parnell's death. His opponent suggested that he hoped to win by combining Parnellite emotion with local Toryism—if so, he seriously miscalculated, as he was well beaten. Another vacancy arose a few weeks later in Waterford City, and here another trial of strength was held, with Michael Davitt as the anti-Parnellite candidate. Feeling ran rather high, and there were many violent incidents; at one point—to Redmond's dismay—Davitt was badly cut on the face. But this time Redmond was victorious, thanks in significant measure, he felt, to the support of the *Waterford News*, owned by C. P. Redmond.[1] Davitt sardonically remarked that the election had been won by 'Terrorism' and 'Toryism'; nevertheless, Redmond was to remain M.P. for Waterford for nearly thirty years, until his death in 1918. The general election of 1892 reduced the Parnellites to a mere nine members—a massive reduction on their position at the time of the party split.

The history of the Parnellite minority of the 1890s has always been overshadowed by the issue of anticlericalism, in part because Parnellism—and Redmond himself personally—attracted some celebrated anticlerical literary intellectuals in the 1890s. Bishop Nulty of Meath was one of the more extreme opponents of the Parnellites on moral grounds. A famous pastoral declared:

> Parnellism, like many great rebellious movements which heresy has from time to time raised against the Church, springs from the roots of sensualism and sin. No man can remain a Catholic so long as he elects to cling to Parnellism. The dying Parnellite himself will hardly dare to face the justice of his Maker till he has been prepared for and anointed by us for the last awful struggle and the terrible judgement that will immediately follow it.[2]

It took a certain courage not to wilt under such pressure. One Parnellite M.P., William Field, confessed: 'They [the Catholic clergy] made social and business matters so bitter that I believe at the time it would have been impossible for us to live in Ireland but for the presence of a large number of Protestants in the community.'[3] Other Parnellites agreed and queried Catholic Ireland's reputation for toleration. Interestingly, though, Redmond took the opposite view: worried Irish Protestants ought to be reassured by the 'spirit of independence' shown by the Parnellite minority—this was their best guarantee of fair play in the future.[4]

Redmond intensely disliked this controversy with his church; little that he said in the period in any way added to its intensity. After one relatively relaxed lunch with the Archbishop of Dublin, William J. Walsh, on 24 February 1895, he had hoped that Parnellite priests would be allowed to give open platform support to Parnellite candidates. This was a step too far—the archbishop wrote quickly to deny his request. Redmond could only reply sadly, if truthfully: 'I entirely disclaim the advocacy of any "views" which would be unworthy of the support of the clergy of my Church.'[5]

The fact remains, however, that Redmond had other important political priorities apart from his relations with the Catholic Church. They have traditionally been neglected. The truth is that anticlericalism—however popular with some of his radical followers—is a shaky foundation on which to build a political strategy, especially in Ireland. It was necessary for him to expand the range of meanings which might be encompassed in a discourse of Parnellite politics after the death of the 'chief' himself. Here Redmond was rather successful; and this was combined with a growing appreciation on all sides of his skills as a parliamentarian. He developed a distinctive approach to the problems faced by Irish nationalists in the 1890s—an approach which, none the less, could be plausibly stated to have roots in the thinking of Parnell. Despite the fact that he had the solid support of less than a dozen Parnellite M.P.s as against 71 anti-Parnellites, Redmond did not feel on this account that he was inhibited from original thinking. He retained, after all, the support of one-third of the Irish electorate. His first great opportunity came with the rejection by the House of Lords of the second Home Rule Bill in 1893. The rejection was hardly a surprise. The eighty-four-year-old Gladstone had always felt that he would need a majority of over one hundred to carry such a controversial measure; in the event, the 'deplorable case of Mr Parnell' reduced it to forty: 'quite insufficient for the purpose of fighting the House of Lords'. It was, therefore, a hopeless cause; and this explained some of Redmond's rhetoric which embarrassed Gladstone during the debates on the measure: 'Redmond's onslaughts on the Bill gave such a handle to the Tories that more than one of them asked what was the good of going on with it, since they had the assurance of so prominent a Nationalist member that it would settle nothing.'[6] But it was in the aftermath of the rejection of the measure that Redmond showed his capacity for original thinking. Understandably, most Irish nationalists were tempted to sustain a particular animus against the undemocratic, unelected elite which had rejected the verdict of the democratically elected House of Commons. Many nationalists were tempted to commit themselves to an alliance with left liberal forces in British politics—this had in any case been part of the texture of much nationalist activity in the 1880s—in order to democratise the British constitution. Redmond, however, held out against a strategy—essentially an alliance of Irish nationalism and British 'democracy'. His reasons were profound and were presented in an important article in *The Nineteenth Century* in November 1894:

> Does anyone really believe that without another revolution, the House of Lords could be abolished within the next fifty years? And does anyone really believe in the possibility of another revolution within the same period directed against a fundamental part of a constitution under which English liberty has been irrevocably established?

The great strong point in Redmond's article is apparent. He insisted on the overriding need to achieve much greater explicit support for Home Rule from both British politicians and the electorate. 'What power has the House of Lords to resist the will of the majority of the people of the United Kingdom in that matter or any other, provided only that the expression of the people's will in Parliament is the result of a clear mandate from the constituencies?' He answered his own question: 'It has none, and what is more has never permanently or even for a long time persisted in the exercise of such a power in the case supposed.'[7]

Why was there ambiguity in the British public mood on Home Rule? Redmond's answer was explicit: there were genuine fears about the treatment of Irish Protestants by a Home Rule movement. Redmond did not share these fears; in 1892 he had written to William Mather, a Lancashire Liberal M.P.: 'As to Ulster, I don't consider any special safeguards necessary at all.'[8] A year later he told the magazine *Black and White* in the course of an interview: 'By her superior intelligence, education and other qualities, she [Ulster] will rise to the top . . . I remember Mr Parnell once saying that, as far as he had read the history of the world, he never knew any nation to rebel except against a *real* grievance, and that real grievance will be absent in this case.'[9] But he acknowledged that, justified or not, these negative perceptions existed. He was here echoing Parnell's great Belfast speech of May 1891 on this topic. Parnell had then said: 'It is undoubtedly true . . . that until the prejudices of the minority, whether reasonable or unreasonable are conciliated . . . Ireland can never enjoy perfect freedom, Ireland can never be united.'[10] Redmond now began to act in precisely this spirit. Unlike mainstream nationalists, he co-operated wholeheartedly with public-spirited Liberal Unionists such as Thomas Sinclair and Thomas Andrews on the Recess Committee of 1895[11] which eventually led to the establishment of the Department of Agriculture in 1899 with Sir Horace Plunkett as its head. Similarly, Redmond joined with the Unionist leader, Colonel E. J. Saunderson, the anti-Parnellite Tim Healy, and the O'Conor Don, who, as we have seen, had been defeated by Willie Redmond in the 1883 Wexford by-election, in signing a circular—not signed by John Dillon, the leader of the anti-Parnellite majority—calling for a conference of Irish parliamentarians designed to put pressure on the government on the issue of Irish taxation levels. Most importantly, when Irish local government was 'democratised' in 1898, effecting (as Redmond put it) 'a social revolution', he argued for a policy of electoral 'toleration': Parnellites should use some of their votes to return public-spirited elements in localities, even if they were not necessarily nationalists.[12] Redmond was to make it clear that the O'Conor Don was a classic case in point in his view. But it was also clear that, unlike other nationalists who claimed that 'all the landlords deserve of Ireland is a single ticket to Holyhead', Redmond was offering an olive branch to all these landlords with any claim to public-spiritedness. One of Parnell's most important parliamentary speeches just before the split had called on the landlords to play a key role in the social regeneration and political leadership of Ireland. Redmond was to repeat these points in parliament himself, in a most significant speech of March 1898. He denounced the origins and history of Irish landlordism—Parnell had been right to challenge the system—but the present generation of landlords were not to blame, a fact which the 'bulk of the Irish people' appreciated:

> After all, these landlords are Irishmen. They are mostly men of education and ability. While we have waged war against a system, I believe the great bulk of the Irish people never at any time desired to drive any class of their fellow countrymen from the shores of Ireland. So far from desiring to ruin them individually, I do not hesitate to say that I believe it would be a wise and blessed thing for Ireland to agree to any financial arrangement by which they could transfer their estates to the people upon such terms as would enable them to retain sufficient, at any rate, of their nominal income to enable them to remain in Ireland to take their proper place among the people. For my part, these are the views that I entertain, and have always entertained, upon this matter.[13]

There were obvious defects in Redmond's approach. He became increasingly hostile in his attitude towards British Liberalism; understandably so, perhaps, as, after Gladstone's retirement from the premiership in 1894, the Liberals cooled in their ardour for Home Rule. Nevertheless, Redmond—unwisely, in the view of close friends—allowed the Parnellite press to pillory 'the British Democrat, the fattest, best clothed, best housed and best paid Democrat in the world'.[14] Redmond's underlying assessment was simple but faulty: he was sure that the Liberals would never again regain power without Nationalist support; there was, therefore, no need to palliate them in any way. The Liberal landslide of 1906 was to prove him wrong. He was also mistaken in his belief that the veto of the House of Lords would survive his active political life; the 1910–11 budget crisis was to prove him wrong here also. The Tories—who were back in government by

1895—on the other hand were treated with surprising kindness. If they repressed Irish nationalism, Redmond said, it would merely strengthen the movement. If—as was more likely—they engaged in reform, then nationalists should co-operate with others in Irish society to assist such reform. It is clear that Redmond's natural conservatism which had inevitably been diluted in the radical 1880s was now reasserting itself in the less turbulent 1890s. It led him to misjudge the trends in British political life, and it also left him exposed when radical agrarianism re-emerged in Ireland in 1898.

In early 1898 William O'Brien launched in Mayo a revived though inevitably rather different Land League type of organisation, the United Irish League. It cannot be said that Redmond was pleased. As Warre B. Wells explained, 'Mr Redmond did not share Mr O'Brien's eagerness to revive the land agitation in its old acute form: his hope was rather for a softening of the class struggle . . . A new agrarian movement such as Mr O'Brien contemplated would, as he saw, destroy the prospect, slight though it was, of converting the Irish gentry to patriotic principles.'[15] But O'Brien's new movement, while never achieving the appeal of the original Land League, had significant areas of success: in particular, many of Redmond's closest political allies in the west (such as John Fitzgibbon and the Hayden family) felt obliged to support the United Irish League in their localities. As a result, O'Brien's United Irish League sapped the independent base of 'Parnellism' and became a force for party unity which Redmond could not ignore—even though it cut across his own political priorities. However, O'Brien was prepared, as a healing gesture, to support a Parnellite such as Redmond for the chair of any reunited party. It was not a course of action which appealed to the principal anti-Parnellite, John Dillon, but it began increasingly to have appeal for John Redmond.

3

CHAIRMAN OF THE PARTY

Redmond's election to the chair of the reunited Irish Parliamentary Party symbolised much of his career. He had a choice between the maintenance of a political strategy in which he profoundly believed—but which was, however, facing the law of diminishing returns—and some form of public pre-eminence and formal victory. In 1900 he chose the latter, rather as in the turbulent 1880s pride and the desire for renown had overridden a natural conservatism and moderation. He allowed himself to be lifted by a tide of squalid intrigue into the chair of the Irish Party—'the country rocked with laughter, but this piece of excellent buffoonery cost Ireland dear'.[1] In 1900 Redmond became chairman, with the important figure of John Dillon as a 'foe'. This would have made life difficult at the best of times, but Dillon was soon to be assisted by the West Belfast Nationalist, Joe Devlin (first elected to parliament for North Kilkenny in 1902), and his secret and increasingly powerful 'organisation of Catholic Freemasonry', the Ancient Order of Hibernians. This made it almost impossible to give any distinctive Redmondite direction to the affairs of the party.

The difficulty of Redmond's position was apparent. Tim Healy, William O'Brien and John Dillon were the three great prickly personalities of post-Parnellite politics. In 1899 Redmond temporarily won O'Brien's support; perhaps more surprisingly, he had managed against all the odds—given Healy's bitterness during the fall of Parnell—to form a bloc also with Healy. (In part, this had been necessitated by the need to find a buyer for the fading Parnellite *Independent* newspaper; Healy's friend, the businessman William Martin Murphy, was almost the only realistic buyer.) Healy therefore looked forward to a Redmond leadership which would be responsive to his own particular concerns; as he briefed his friends on the *New York Times,* the party's leadership would now be in the hands of a 'commission' in which he obviously intended to figure.[2] O'Brien, however, also believed he could exercise decisive influence over Redmond. Had O'Brien's United Irish League, he asked, not disrupted Redmond's policy of social peace in the countryside? Had O'Brien not managed to seduce key Parnellite lieutenants away from Redmond's side? Surely Redmond would appreciate who was the real master in rural Ireland? Yet Dillon, for all that his cool and chilly personality had alienated both O'Brien and Healy, retained the intense personal loyalty of, at the very least, one-third of the party's M.P.s. Redmond clearly calculated that this gave Dillon an effective veto over party policy. Healy was rapidly driven out of the party despite Redmond's efforts to retain him; perhaps more importantly, the growing Murphyite *Independent* press empire responded by treating Redmond with persistent coolness and thus made the new chairman over-dependent on the *Freeman's Journal* group, which was controlled by Thomas Sexton, a close friend of Dillon. For two years Redmond's relationship with O'Brien was closer—in the main because of his intrinsic political strength.

But as the United Irish League spread out of its smallholding Connacht base it became—as the Land League of 1879–82 had become—a more complex national organisation, and more responsive to the interests of strong farmers. O'Brien tried desperately to maintain its radicalism and militancy, and he was given formal public support by Redmond; in private matters were, however, rather different. By August 1902 Redmond made it perfectly clear that he was anxious to control and limit agrarian militancy. This warning seems to have helped to predispose an exhausted O'Brien towards a change of policy; when landlord spokesmen suggested a conference on the land question with tenant leaders, O'Brien and Redmond—encouraged by hints of Tory government financial generosity—threw themselves whole-heartedly into the process of dialogue in December 1902. By the autumn of 1903 O'Brien and Redmond could point to the Wyndham Act as the fruit of their consensual labours—the 'greatest measure since the Union', said Redmond. In essence, the most divisive issue of nineteenth-century Irish history had, in principle, been solved by the British government's strong financial support for peasant proprietorship. The implication was clear for William O'Brien: the old slogans of rural class conflict were irrelevant, and dialogue with those traditionally outside the ranks of popular nationalism was now the only way forward. In his heart, Redmond agreed profoundly—he had, after all, been inclined to such views as early as the 1890s—but again he had to check O'Brien. In part influenced by the negative publicity arising from the price he had sought, under the Wyndham Act, for some land he had inherited from his uncle, General Redmond; but principally because he felt weakened simply by John Dillon's vocal opposition—backed by the *Freeman*— Redmond, refused to allow O'Brien to impose his new politics on the party. Dillon spoke for that large bloc of Irish M.P.s who had made their reputation in the days of agrarian agitation—and this was a substantial majority—and who now, in many cases, simply could not accept that the land question was in some sense solved. In any case, the Wyndham Act, far-reaching though it was—two-thirds of Irish farmers were to own their own land by 1914—could not deal with many of the problems of Ireland's rural poor and land-hungry. These have-nots could still be mobilised by party activists, as the ranch war of 1906–10 was clearly to show. But this time there was a novel problem: as the 'alien' landlords became less and less significant in the countryside, a renewed bout of agrarian class conflict was much more likely to pit the interests of Catholic nationalist farmer against those of another Catholic nationalist farmer.[3]

In the autumn of 1904, partly to raise money and partly as a relief from these tensions, Redmond went on a speaking tour of the United States. Here his tone was, unsurprisingly, rather strident; he told *Harper's Magazine*: 'How can there be any progress when a little group of ignorant Englishmen make our laws?'[4] Yet Redmond's private correspondence with J. C. Walsh, the editor of the Irish Party's American journal, shows clearly that he believed that not only was there 'progress' at this juncture, but even a 'revolution' in Irish social conditions.[5]

Unionists seized on some of Redmond's more intemperate speeches and contrasted them with his tone in the House of Commons. He was, in effect, challenged to repeat some of his American rhetoric in parliament; it was a challenge he decided to take up. He told the House in the spring of 1905:

They regarded the government of their country by this Parliament as a usurpation; they denied the validity and deputed the moral binding force of the Act of Union. They demanded self-government, not as a favour, but as a right; they based their demand, not upon grievances, but upon the inherent and unalienable right of the Irish nation to govern itself. They declared plainly that they would rather be governed badly by their own Parliament than well by that Assembly . . .

If he believed that there was the smallest reasonable chance of success, he would have no hesitation in advising his fellow countrymen to endeavour to end the present system by armed revolt.[6]

One comment on his speech is of particular interest. It came from Sir Robert Anderson, an obsessive but well-informed member of the intelligence service, who was a bitter opponent of Irish nationalism. Drawing attention to Redmond's speech, he observed with a mixture of exasperation and insight:

The character of the speaker lends weight to these words. Not only is he the leader of the Nationalist party, but personally he differs from most of his colleagues in two respects, namely: first, he is a gentleman and never indulges in coarse or offensive language; and secondly, he is a sensible man who avoids the style of oratory which Americans call 'flapdoodle'. If all Parnellites were men of the type of J. E. Redmond, Home Rule might not spell disaster. But such men are few, and they would soon be pushed aside.[7]

The Liberal landslide electoral victory of 1906 offered a potential way out of these sterile exchanges. But it was again to prove a rather difficult operation.

The devolution crisis of 1906–7 appeared to present an action replay of the Wyndham Act controversy. Here again was the chance to work with the grain of government policy rather than against. The Liberal government in 1906 felt unable to offer Home Rule, but was prepared to offer a far-reaching measure of devolution on an all-Ireland basis. O'Brien was attracted to the scheme because it allowed an opportunity for nationalists and unionists to work together; Redmond seems again to have been open to this argument,[8] but in the end he had to accept that it was impossible for the Irish Party to accept anything less than the full measure of legislative Home Rule on the Gladstone model.

Once again the impression persisted that organised nationalist public opinion—as expressed in the nationalist convention of 21 May 1907—was more militant and less conciliatory than the party leader.[9]

In particular, Redmond was obviously ill-at-ease with the renewed cattle-driving campaign which characterised the ranch war of 1906–10. His principal reason was clear enough: cattle-driving was unpopular with those English Liberals whose support for Home Rule was essential. Any hint of rural lawlessness or cruelty to animals undermined the positive image of a respectable nationalism which Redmond was trying to generate. But there was another problem. The land war of 1879–82 had been characterised by a significant degree of disunity on the Land League side; nevertheless, the overriding message was one of hostility to the claims of 'alien' landlordism. The ranch war, on the other hand, was inevitably more confusing. A remarkably high proportion of the principal leaders of the ranch war either were or became graziers or were closely related to graziers—John Hayden, John Fitzgibbon and Patrick McKenna all belong in this category. Others were guilty of attempting to call off the struggle against the graziers when it affected the interest of friends, associates or potential supporters in internal U.I.L. disputes—W. J. Duffy, 'Farmer' Hogan and David Sheehy fell into this category. Even the paid organisers of the U.I.L., who were traditionally more radical than the elected politicians, harboured their black sheep—T. A. Morris, the enthusiastic western organiser, was to be embarrassed by a cattle-drive on his own farm.[10] As one militant ranch warrior, Lawrence Ginnell, admitted, many ranchers were 'excellent nationalists'.

Fearful of growing divisions, perhaps understandably, Redmond came to exalt the unity of party above any other strategic consideration. At Longford in September 1907 he was very clear on this point. He was glad to welcome any Irishman, 'of any creed, class or politics . . . who chooses to come in and give assistance on any Irish question'.[11] 'But', he added, 'I am bound to honestly say this, that my profound conviction is, that in the long run we must rely upon our own movement, and that if we allow it to grow slack or be broken, or the action of the Irish parliamentary party is suspended, that it is not worth a price of salt. The moral I point, therefore, is this: support your party, insist upon its being a united and disciplined party acting as one man.' The O'Brienite *Irish People* disagreed with this emphasis: 'A united party of power, strength and independence is an important factor but not the only one.'[12] In 1908 Redmond attempted a reconciliation with O'Brien and Healy, but it floundered in 1909 over differing responses to the Birrell Land Act.

Despite this, in 1909 Redmond's political fortunes seemed to improve. It appeared that he could put to one side a ranch war for which he had little sympathy, and concentrate on high politics and the renewed prospect of Home Rule. David Lloyd George, the Chancellor of the Exchequer, introduced his radical 'People's Budget'. To some degree the measure was controversial in Ireland—not least because it imposed new whiskey and land taxes—and the eventual decision to give it support required careful justification.[13] But what mattered most was the hostility of the House of Lords, which decided to break with constitutional precedent and reject the budget, thereby bringing down the government and provoking a great conflict between the two Houses of Parliament. The general elections of January and December 1910 had almost identical results and left the Irish Parliamentary Party holding the balance of power at Westminster. Redmond now suddenly gained a stature similar to that of Parnell in 1885–6. In theory, he could make or break governments. Many who had dismissed him as a second-rater now discovered that he possessed political skills of a high order. Prime Minister Asquith, like Gladstone in 1886, was quick to respond: in 1912 he introduced the third Home Rule Bill. Redmond, it seemed, was in charge, the dominant player in a new political game.

There was, of course, a deep irony here. Redmond's success was due precisely to methods and a strategy—an alliance with radicals to break the House of Lords—which he had decried in the mid-1890s. At that time he had declared the policy to be a futile distraction—a harmful substitute for the real policy, one which stressed the primacy of winning over Protestants and Unionists in Ireland. Naturally, those outside nationalist ranks were not slow to remind Redmond of his apparent inconsistency. He was reminded of his earlier argument that the opposition of the House of Lords to Home Rule reflected a more generalised sense of uneasiness with the population at large: 'Nobody knows better than Mr Redmond that if, in [the general election of] 1895, a clear majority . . . had been returned in favour of Home Rule, the measure, or a similar one would have been passed by the House of Lords.' It was argued that Redmond was in reality afraid even before 1912 that a veto by the House of Lords of Home Rule 'would be affirmed, as in 1895, on an appeal to the constituencies'.[14] The *Freeman's Journal* (18 Dec. 1912) replied on Redmond's behalf that circumstances had changed: 'It would require a revolution, Mr Redmond said fourteen years ago. He was quite right, it did require a revolution to create the opportunity and the Lords have obligingly provided the revolution.' This was a perceptive comment, but one circumstance had not changed: the vast majority of Irish Protestants were as deeply suspicious of the Home Rule project in 1910 as they had been in 1895. In one respect, matters were worse, as one of the more powerful Unionist leaflets, *Nationalist Fair Play*, pointed out. Redmond, it recalled, had argued in 1898 that—following the democratisation of Irish local government—Protestants would receive the fullest toleration. In fact, by 1912 only 15 out of 703 Irish county councillors outside Ulster were Unionist. More to the point was the record of these councils in salaried appointments: fourteen of them had not made one single Protestant appointment, it was claimed, while five others had made only one each. Nationalists, of course, made similar claims about northern councils—in particular that of Belfast. But there still remained a personal question for Redmond: 'On the face of a record like this, is it any wonder that Protestants put no faith in Redmond's professions of toleration? Even if he is perfectly sincere, he could not carry out his promises as he failed to carry out those in 1898.'[15]

But Redmond's mind was no longer focused on such matters. Instead he preferred to allow his always latent liberal imperialism to flower. Two interviews he gave at this time were particularly revealing. In May 1908 Redmond was interviewed by A. G. Gardiner: 'Our stake in the Empire is too large for us to be detached from it,' he declared; 'the Irish people peopled the waste places of Greater Britain. Our roots are in the Imperial as well as the national.'[16] And in October 1910 he told the New York correspondent of the *Daily Express*: 'We do not demand such complete autonomy as the British self-governing colonies possess, for we are willing to abide by any fiscal system . . . enacted by the British government . . . Once we receive home rule, we shall demonstrate our imperial loyalty beyond question.'[17] What did it all mean? Only time would tell.

4

AN IMPERIAL NATIONALISM?

As early as November 1886 Redmond had insisted in a lecture given at the Rotunda, Dublin, that 'there are no two nations in Ireland today, and secondly, that all the history of the past disproves the assertion that Catholic Irishmen ever were guilty of religious persecution and all the experience of the present shows them to be incapable of either intolerance or bigotry'.[1] He never abandoned these general convictions; of course, the difficulty lay in the fact that Ulster Unionists firmly believed both that there were two nations in Ireland and that Irish Catholics were indeed perfectly capable of intolerance and bigotry. While other Parnellites tended to argue that the experience of the early 1890s bore this last point out, Redmond did not. Instead he had argued that Protestants ought to be heartened by the doughty independent spirit of the Parnellite minority. Redmond had nevertheless been prepared to make real sacrifices for his policy of toleration in the 1890s. In the 1900s, however, he began increasingly to see party unity as an end in itself; after the Dillonite 'Swinford revolt' of 1903 he had perhaps little choice. When the McCann affair erupted in 1911, Redmond was uncharacteristically silent, even though it raised all the issues which had been at the core of his Rotunda address in 1886. To Irish Protestants it seemed as if a Protestant wife was abandoned, and her children spirited away in obedience to the Vatican *Ne temere* decree of 1908. Protestant Ireland was moved by 'pity for the poor young Presbyterian girl who trusted the "plighted troth" of a Roman Catholic, and as a consequence now finds herself husbandless, childless, homeless, and penniless'. The Catholic priest who told Mrs McCann that her marriage was invalid became *in absentia* a core element in Protestant demonology. Redmond's silence on the subject was less than impressive. The Rev. Dudley Fletcher, D.D., of Coolbanagher, a prominent Church of Ireland clergyman, wrote: 'Mr Redmond has missed a grand opportunity of furthering the Home Rule cause. Had he, in the name of his party, and of the Irish Roman Catholics generally expressed a few kindly words of sympathy and pity for this poor heart-broken woman, he would have won the hearts of Irish Protestants, and taken the most bitter sting out of Home Rule. As it is, the treatment which Mrs McCann has received is becoming every day a more and more serious obstacle to the passing of a Home Rule Bill.'[2]

These must have been personally sensitive matters for Redmond. His mother had been a Protestant until her marriage. His own second wife was an English Protestant. Yet he never conceded that there was any possible validity in the religious fears of Ulster Protestants. As the third Home Rule crisis unfolded, it became clear that Redmond remained committed to the views he had first enunciated in 1886. In one article published in the *Review of Reviews* in November 1912 he insisted with some fatuity that 'there was no Ulster question'.[3] Then in an elegant essay for a Canadian academic periodical he argued that the essence of Unionism was hostility towards the notion of equality of treatment for Irish Catholics. He admitted that in the House of Commons the Unionists denied this, but argued that the historical record spoke for itself.[4]

There was an element of truth in this analysis. Nevertheless, the lack of insight into the intensity of Protestant fears—and the objective reasons for them—helps to both explain and vitiate Redmond's strategy. Instead of acknowledging the seriousness of the problem, Redmond, now armed with the 'balance of power' in the House of Commons, tried to make the cabinet do his bidding and deliver an all-Ireland Home Rule settlement—even though, as early as February 1912 when the third Home Rule Bill was introduced in parliament, the Prime Minister, H. H. Asquith, and other leading figures in the cabinet such as David Lloyd George and Winston Churchill had the gravest doubts about the viability of such a policy.[5] Lloyd George appears to have favoured some scheme of Ulster exclusion without a time limit from the start.[6] But the cabinet's superficial willingness to follow Redmond's agenda infuriated Ulster Unionists, who now began a mass-based popular resistance to Home Rule which—borrowing its tactics from Fenianism—attempted to prevail against the British government by a mixture of rhetoric and the threat of force.

Outside the sphere of purely religious fears, it would not be fair to say that Redmond was indifferent to Unionist concerns. Home Rule was, he said, above all a measure of democratisation: 'Dublin Castle . . . that horrible system—anti-Irish, unrepresentative, centralised, bureaucratic—which misgoverned, tortured and ruined Ireland crumbles instantly into dust.'[7] But for Unionists, of course, the key question then was: who was to dominate the new institutions of government? He tried to meet Unionist fears here by stressing the continued supremacy of the Westminster parliament and the continued links with London and the Empire; most important of all, he argued that the Irish Party, its object achieved, would wither away:

> The very moment Home Rule is granted it will become the highest interest of the Irish nation to safeguard that constitution and to work it with moderation and success. It will instantly become the highest interest of the Irish people to cultivate the most friendly possible relations with Great Britain, and it will become the interest of Ireland, for the first time, I am afraid, in her history, to do all in her power to promote the unity, prosperity and welfare of the Empire. My own firm belief is that, in a very short period of time indeed, all the old lines of party division in Ireland will disappear. The Home Rule party, as you have known it, will disappear; it will be *functus officio*, because the object for which it was called into existence, and for which it worked, will have been accomplished. It will break up, and new parties will instantly spring into existence.[8]

But if the Irish Party withered away, what would fill the power vacuum? Redmond's argument was both surprising and deceptively simple. It would be the well-heeled upper classes who had previously been estranged from the nationalist movement. The method of involving them was simple—they would constitute the nominated second chamber: 'I want the Irish second Chamber from the very start to be crowded with men who have not been partisans of the National Party in the past at all.'[9] This led D. P. Moran of *The Leader* to observe bitterly: 'Is the end of home rule to be that the Unionists are to run the country?'[10]

During the committee stage of the Home Rule Bill Redmond also did what he could to offer a measure of reassurance to Unionist cultural concerns.[11] It is perhaps not surprising that he was prepared to offer cast-iron assurances that a Home Rule parliament would not interfere with the working of Trinity College, Dublin, or the Queen's University of Belfast. On the other hand, he could do little to placate Unionist fears about the role of compulsory Irish in schools or public appointments; on these issues the Gaelic League had mobilised public opinion—or at any rate had created a new piety within the nationalist political class—which made it impossible for Redmond to be flexible.

As the crisis deepened, in February 1914 the Unionist leader, Sir Edward Carson—worried perhaps by the militancy of his supporters in the Ulster Volunteers—made a statesmanlike speech calling for his 'nationalist fellow countrymen' to try to win over the Ulster Unionists by sympathetic understanding rather than political manoeuvre. The speech affected Redmond deeply; he started to talk of a compromise based on county option, whereby counties with a Unionist majority could opt out of the Home Rule scheme—but only on a temporary six-year basis. It took an effort to go even this far: Joe Devlin in particular was doing everything to hold Redmond to an Irish unity position. Nevertheless, Redmond's close aide, Stephen Gwynn, felt that the Irish leader had not gone quite far enough in pursuit of reconciliation. In a striking passage, Gwynn wrote:

> Redmond probably believed that the opinion of Nationalists could not be brought to consent to abandonment of the time limit. If so, he probably underrated, then as always, the influence he possessed. It is always best to persuade Irishmen that if you are going to do a thing you should do it 'decently'. What is more a real effect could have been produced in much opinion in Ulster by saying to Ulster: 'Stay out if you like, and come in when you like. When you come in, you will be more than welcome . . .' If a clear proposal of local option by counties without time limit had been put before Parliament and the electorate, I do not think our position in Ireland would have been worse than it was made by the proposal of temporary exclusion, and it would have been greatly strengthened in Parliament and the United Kingdom.[12]

This is a very serious argument, coming as it does from the pen of one of Redmond's most trusted and talented colleagues. The argument is a simple one; by offering some form of county option, Redmond had already compromised himself with important sections of nationalist opinion, yet, by insisting on a time limit, he gained no compensating credit from those Unionists—and there were a significant number in the Ulster Unionist leadership—who wished to avoid an open conflict of arms. Worse still, the argument focused on the time-limit issue and not on the other area where the Unionist argument was weakest on democratic grounds—in particular the desire to hold on to counties like Fermanagh and Tyrone where there were slender nationalist majorities. The problem of these counties was to be exacerbated by the failure to reach a compromise in March 1914; in April both the so-called Curragh 'mutiny', when it became clear that the British army could not be used to smash 'Carsonism', and the Larne gun-running took place. Both events greatly strengthened Unionist hardliners and, in particular, made any Unionist concession on Fermanagh and Tyrone almost impossible. The Buckingham Palace Conference—called for 21–24 July 1914 as a last desperate attempt to broker a deal—floundered on the future status of these two counties as well as the time-limit issue. Carson later recalled a poignant event as the Buckingham Palace Conference collapsed: 'I remember Mr John Redmond coming up to me and saying "For the sake of the old time on circuit let us have a good shake hands."'[13]

There is something of an irony in this exchange. Carson's commitment to the Irish bar was a deep one—'the happiest times of all my life were at T.C.D. and the Irish bar'[14]—while Redmond's enthusiasm had been rather more lukewarm. Nevertheless, Redmond clearly felt the strength of that 'old personal tie' formed at the Irish bar, a 'true centre of intercourse between men of varying political and religious beliefs'.[15]

Immediately after this encounter Redmond and Dillon, in an afternoon meeting with Asquith in Downing Street, finally and all too belatedly dropped the time-limit idea. As Professor Bentley Brinkerhoff Gilbert has concluded, 'Exclusion thus would be permanent. So the Liberals at the end had retreated to the point at which Lloyd George had urged them to start when the bill was drawn up.'[16]

But the exponents of direct action on the nationalist side—where the Irish Volunteers expanded and responded in proportion to Ulster Volunteer militancy—were now beginning to influence the agenda in a way deleterious to Redmond's strategy. Two days later, in a nationalist *riposte* to Larne, the Howth gun-running took place, ending in confrontation with the police and loss of life in Dublin.

Some felt that Ireland was sliding into civil war, but suddenly a massive external development—the outbreak of the First World War—overshadowed the factional conflicts on the island. It was to provide Redmond with his personal moment of truth and his greatest political challenge. He resolved to give a new meaning to the old nationalist cliché 'England's difficulty is Ireland's opportunity' and made clear his support for Britain's struggle against Germany. Redmond's speech in the House of Commons when Sir Edward Grey announced his government's intention to go to war with Germany was, in fact, a rather cautious if effective intervention. He offered simply that Ireland would be guarded by the Ulster Volunteers and the Irish Volunteers and that Britain might withdraw her troops. It has been argued that Redmond's speech was unpremeditated and that he was unwisely impelled to make a generous move by the emotion of the moment. It is true that Redmond made some kind of show of impulsiveness in last-minute consultation with colleagues J. P. Hayden and T. P. O'Connor; John Dillon, perhaps significantly, was absent in Ireland. But the bulk of the evidence points in a different direction. It seems rather more likely that Redmond, having received Asquith's commitment to place Home Rule on the statute book, then, and only then, decided to act. This was certainly the view of Michael MacDonagh, who covered the moment as a working journalist. MacDonagh later observed:

> It ought to have been clear to his colleagues that . . . he came to the House of Commons with his speech carefully prepared and written out. He made no disguise of the fact—as I noted at the time—that he was reading it from half sheets of notepaper. Presumably, he was determined, on this critical occasion, to be leader in fact as well as in name.[17]

Redmond's strategy, combined with the depth of the crisis, allowed the government to impose a compromise on Ireland: Home Rule became law in September 1914, but its implementation was to be postponed until after the end of the war—a war Redmond expected to last but a year—and until after new legislation had been enacted to deal with the problem of Ulster.

Redmond in the meantime threw himself enthusiastically into support of the British war effort—to the dismay of some of his more cautious lieutenants. He urged Irishmen in his Woodenbridge speech in September 1914 to join the British army and to fight 'wherever the firing-line extends, in defence of right, of freedom and of religion in this war'. At first this policy was successful. The Irish Volunteers split, but 170,000 men remained loyal to Redmond, while only 10,000 men supported the more radical nationalist leadership of Eoin MacNeill and his colleagues. It was, however, this smaller group which was to provide the nucleus for the insurrection of Easter 1916.

What was Redmond's reasoning, and why did the bulk of nationalist Ireland support it? Redmond pointed out that constitutional nationalists had always insisted that there was no strategic risk to Britain in conceding Home Rule; here was the opportunity to act with honour and prove that this had been a sincere and truthful argument. The consequences of reneging on it were incalculable. Redmond hoped too that a common struggle in the armed forces would bring Irish Catholic and Protestant closer together. But, if not, he felt sure that nationalist Ireland could not allow the Unionists to win all the credit for sacrifice in the British cause. Some form of partition was by now inevitable, but questions of the size of the partitioned area and the form of government were still open. Nationalists could not afford to lose their bargaining position by staying at home: 'I say, as sensible men and fair women, put yourselves in the position of Englishmen . . . If it were proved to you that nationalist Irishmen had broken faith and that Ireland had refused to do her duty and the only men who had done their duty were the Ulster volunteers, what would you do? You know very well what an ordinary man would do under the circumstances. He would say I will stand by the man who stood by me.'[18] Finally, Redmond felt a strong personal sympathy for the plight of Catholic Belgium, where a niece lived as a nun. For a considerable time these arguments, while not received with universal enthusiasm, seemed to carry the day.

Between the outbreak of war in 1914 and the Easter Rising of 1916 Redmondite or Irish Party candidates won all five of the contested by-elections in Ireland; in short, the party saw off all radical nationalist challenges. Nevertheless, there is clear evidence of a growing weakness of the United Irish League's structures. In general, Redmond could find more satisfaction in the three rural results than the urban ones. But even in rural areas there was evidence of a corresponding low level of involvement in the party's apparatus. This was due in significant measure to the fading resonance of the land question; it was also partly due to the absence of many of the best young Redmondites at the front. But when all is said and done, it is evident that before the Easter Rising in 1916 Redmond retained the support of the majority of Irish nationalists, even though matters had become decidedly more difficult after Carson entered the cabinet in May 1915. Redmond had been offered a place in the cabinet at the same time, but had felt that nationalist principle obliged him to refuse; actually the decision was not quite so simple. Redmond had himself argued before the war that Irish M.P.s should take British cabinet posts after Home Rule was granted. When the offer came, Home Rule was, at least, on the statute book; might he not have stretched a point and served in the government and thus preserved its bipartisan—in Irish terms— nature? Interestingly, the influential radical nationalist polemicist D. P. Moran believed that Redmond's self-denial was a mistake; by refusing Asquith's offer, Redmond retained responsibility for the support of the British war effort without any control of its direction—in particular where its direction touched on Irish sensitivities.

Redmond always insisted that the War Office simply did not know how to mobilise Irish patriotism in the cause of the war effort—indeed, that the War Office persistently snubbed nationalist sentiment—but he was now passing up the opportunity to exercise influence in this matter at the highest level. But despite all these difficulties, Redmond could justifiably feel, on the eve of the Easter Rising, that he retained the confidence of the great majority of Irish nationalists.

AFTER THE EASTER RISING

Redmond was caught off guard by the rising in April 1916. As he openly admitted, he had advised Birrell that there was no real danger and had thus contributed to the culture of complacency in Dublin Castle. At bottom, Redmond had found it hard to take the revolutionaries with any degree of seriousness. He did not guess at the sway which might be exercised over men's minds by an almost mystical belief which disdained to count with practicalities.[1]   On 27 April, when parliament reassembled, Redmond expressed the feeling of 'detestation and horror'[2] with which he and his colleagues—except John Dillon, who spoke sympathetically of the motivation of the insurgents, though to little avail—regarded events in Dublin.   Alexander Sullivan, who was a resolute opponent of Sinn Féin, observed that this 'pronouncement was mean and halting'.[3]   There is no doubt that Redmond regarded the execution of three prominent signatories to the Proclamation of the Irish Republic (Pearse, Clarke and MacDonagh) as 'just'.   Nevertheless, he begged the government not to act with 'undue hardship or severity' in dealing with mere followers: 'Let them, in the name of God, not add this to the wretched, miserable memories of the Irish people . . .'[4]

In May 1916 Asquith's severely jolted government authorised Lloyd George to initiate a new round of discussions to see if a settlement was possible.   Both Carson and Redmond did their utmost to achieve a viable compromise, and for a brief moment it appeared that an agreement could be achieved on the basis of six-county exclusion and an ill-defined period of partition. Redmond argued for, and apparently won, acceptance of the principle of the temporary exclusion of six counties, but then found that the government was insisting on an explicitly permanent exclusion.   Redmond bitterly told the House of Commons on 24 July:

> Some tragic fatality seems to dog the footsteps of the government in all their dealing with Ireland . . . They have disregarded every advice we tendered to them, and now in the

end, having got us to induce our people to make a tremendous sacrifice and to agree to the temporary exclusion of these Ulster counties, they throw this agreement to the winds, and they have taken the surest means to accentuate every possible danger and difficulty in the Irish situation.[5]

Stephen Gwynn summarised the implications with great force:

That day really finished the constitutional party and overthrew Redmond's power. We had incurred the very great odium of accepting even temporary partition—and a partition which, owing to this arbitrary extension of areas, could not be justified on any ground of principle; we had involved with us many men who voted for that acceptance on the faith of Redmond's assurance that that government was bound by their written words, and now we were thrown over.[6]

Carson had got the best of the deal, but it is clear that he too was genuinely uneasy about the consequences for Redmond's influence within nationalist Ireland.

In early 1917 the government made another desperate bid to achieve an Irish settlement. In his introduction to parliament the proposal to establish an Irish Convention which would be representative of the principal political interests in the country, Lloyd George, now Prime Minister, outlined the thinking which underpinned the new departure:

I cannot help thinking after witnessing repeated failures by several governments to solve this question that this is probably the dominant reason that the proposals all emanated not from the country chiefly concerned but from British governments . . . Therefore, we propose that Ireland should try her own hand at hammering out an instrument of government for her own people.[7]

As Redmond had put it, the model was one in which the patient must minister to himself; in effect this meant the production of a new constitution for the future government of Ireland with only one restriction: that Ireland remain within the Empire—a restriction which, of course, of itself almost guaranteed a Sinn Féin boycott, even though the government genuinely hoped that there would be Sinn Féin representation and took the risk of an amnesty policy in order to facilitate that objective.

The speeches on the establishment of the Irish Convention seemed to indicate a growing understanding between Redmond and Carson. Redmond approached the issue of the composition of the Convention in a generous fashion: 'I desire a full and fair representation of every class, creed, party and interest, with this exception—that I desire most heartily to see the Unionists in that assembly with a larger representation than they would be entitled to by the test of mere proportionate numbers in the community.'[8] The *Freeman's Journal* commented in support: 'The Irish leader's eloquent and moving speech expressed the traditional spirit of Irish Nationalism, as it has been inspired by its apostles in the past—from Grattan to Davis, and from Davis to Parnell. His statement is the final answer to those who have represented the Irish Nationalist Party as a dictatorial, arrogant Party, eager to impose their ideas upon all who differed from them and to admit no counsel as to the interests of the nation.'[9] On behalf of the Ulster Unionists, Sir John Lonsdale made a rather fearful speech: 'To my mind the real motive of the Nationalist party is to be found in the hope that they will be able to force Ulster into the Home Rule scheme against her will.'[10]

Carson, however, called for a more open-minded approach. He regretted Redmond's failure to win his party's support for a compromise in 1916, but he did so with an interesting aside: 'I think, very likely, if Redmond had been able at that time to persuade his friends to accept that solution we might be very much forwarder now in the general union of the whole of Ireland. That is my belief. I believe the moment you shake hands over anything as a step forward to a more general union you'll go further than you ever thought you would.'[11]

The Convention itself was a unique and in certain respects inspiring experience. In its early phase Redmond achieved a kind of apotheosis, finding an expressiveness of tone among an assembly of representative Irishmen he had never quite managed in the House of Commons. Even the chronically suspicious Ulster Unionists indicated that they were willing to have Redmond as chairman; though in the end Redmond, along with others, decided, perhaps unwisely, that Sir Horace Plunkett should hold this post. Some of the sources of misunderstanding between north and south were removed. Unionists, who had expected to find that the provincial worthies of the Irish Party were explosive agrarian radicals, found instead cautious, respectful and rather taciturn small businessmen. Nationalists found men of quality and learning on the Ulster Unionist side—men of whose existence they had been completely unaware. There was even a calm discussion between Colonel Wallace, the Grand Master of the Orange Order, and the most senior Catholic clergy on the thorny issue of *Ne temere*.[12]

These remarkable moments, if they had come earlier, might have benignly changed the course of Irish history. But in 1917 they were overshadowed by the surge of support away from the Irish Party and towards Sinn Féin. As Redmond's close ally Stephen Gwynn admitted, this greatly reduced the incentive for Unionists to make a deal with Redmond. In February and May 1917 the Irish Party suffered, in North Roscommon and South Longford respectively, major though narrow electoral defeats in rural nationalist heartlands, defeats which were the harbingers of its eclipse in late 1918. Then, worst of all, in June 1917 Major Willie Redmond, M.P., was fatally wounded while leading his men of the 5th Battalion of the Royal Irish Regiment in the victorious battle for the Messines Ridge; he was picked up by an Ulster Division ambulance and carried to an Ulster Division field hospital, but never recovered consciousness. The manner of Willie's death, and indeed that of other Redmondites, made a marked impression on the British political elite—erstwhile opponents like Bonar Law and Austen Chamberlain were deeply moved—and even on tough Ulster Unionists (like the Craig brothers) but not on nationalist Ireland. It chose to elect a prominent Sinn Féin leader, Eamon de Valera, for Willie's old seat in East Clare on 10 July. Sinn Féin's most potent slogan was the suggestion that a vote for the Irish Party was a vote to put every able-bodied man of military age into khaki. Then, shortly afterwards, de Valera's campaign manager and 1916 veteran, Thomas Ashe, a former National School teacher, was arrested; Ashe went on hunger-strike and was forcibly fed with fatal results. It did not help matters that Redmond's son-in-law, Max Green, was chairman of the General Prisons Board and involved in key decisions concerning the Ashe case. At the coroner's inquest, under questioning from Tim Healy, K.C., acting for Ashe's family, he refused to divulge sensitive information, saying 'I don't think it is in the King's interest to answer', to the sound of much derisive laughter in the courtroom.[13]

Redmond did his best to retain nationalist credibility in the
face of these sapping events. On 23 October 1917 he moved a
resolution in the House of Commons deploring the government's
coercive policy; a risk had been taken in the amnesty for Sinn
Féin prisoners, he acknowledged, but 'they took no risks compa-
rable to the absolute certainty of disaster if the opposite course
had been adopted'.[14] Instead a policy of provocation and irrita-
tion had been pursued: for example, a proclamation had been
issued prohibiting Swedish gymnastics. Worst of all had been the
treatment of Sinn Féin prisoners by the authorities: unnecessary
arrests for purely rhetorical excesses had been followed by rapid
releases under the threat of hunger-strike in the wake of the Ashe
affair. These developments outside the Convention sapped its
importance. Mainstream nationalist Ireland was clearly in the
process of being captured by Sinn Féin. In one ugly symbolic
incident, Redmond was personally assaulted on the streets of
Dublin by a crowd of young Sinn Féiners.[15]

Meanwhile the Unionists could now see no rationale for a
compromise with nationalism. The one argument which might
have told with them—the need to assist the war effort—was being
subverted. The *Northern Whig* noted: 'There is a great need for
clear thinking at the present time. If a Parliament was established
in Dublin tomorrow it would be a Parliament ruled and
controlled by Germany's allies in this country.'[16] In February
1918 Sinn Féin was defeated by the Irish Party in the South
Armagh by-election; it was, in part, a defeat for de Valera's
dogmatic, threatening attitude towards Unionists: 'They must
either be in Ireland or out of it.'[17] De Valera had laid great stress
on the importance of the campaign: 'I say we are ready to put
Ireland's honour in the hands of Armagh.'[18] Armagh, fortunately
for the Irish Party, was unwilling to play its allotted role. The
victory, significant in its way though it was, however, came too late
to give real comfort to Redmond.

Redmond's Convention policy was a simple one: to mollify
moderate Irish Unionist opinion by offering it a disproportionate
influence within a Home Rule Ireland. He had considerable
success with southern Unionists, but much more difficulty with
the Ulster Unionists who attended. It was Redmond's hope to
attempt to isolate the hardline elements within Unionism;

however, this element of strategy floundered because of divisions in the nationalist side at the Convention. In order to secure an agreement with the southern Unionists, Redmond was prepared to downplay economic nationalism; in particular he was prepared to postpone a decision on whether or not the new Irish parliament should control customs and excise. But a strong nationalist minority headed by Joe Devlin and including three of the four Catholic bishops at the Convention—and backed strongly from without by Convention member William Martin Murphy's *Independent* group of newspapers—refused to accept any such compromise. A strong position on the tariff issue suddenly became a symbol of nationalist integrity, a sort of compensation for the reverses suffered on partition.

The drift of economic thinking within the Redmondite camp had been away from economic nationalism; this was partly because Ireland now benefited from generous British social reform, such as old-age pensions, and partly because of the growing sense of the strength of the economic ties between Ireland and Britain. As the *Freeman's Journal* put it in an important editorial on 'Our Economic Relationship' (14 April 1917), 'We question if there is a single Irish product, with the exception perhaps of flax, to which free access to the British market is not of vital importance . . . No trade measure for many years caused such feeling in Ireland as the restraints imposed upon Irish cattle exports to Great Britain owing to the alleged continued existence of foot and mouth disease among the Irish herds.' In the *Freeman*'s view, the 'demand for reasonable fiscal liberty and the power of industrial development' and taxation had been so 'misrepresented' by opponents of Home Rule that 'people might be led to believe that the first use an Irish parliament would make of its powers would be to begin "openly and undisguisedly" a tariff war with England', utterly indifferent to the interdependence of the trade and economic connection of the two countries. But this sort of relaxed thinking was increasingly under attack in nationalist circles. Sir Horace Plunkett, chairman of the Irish Convention, recorded with exasperation in March 1918 a revealing conversation on the tariff issue with Bishop MacRory of Down and Connor: 'He admitted to me that the principle for which he was fighting had only become a principle of Irish policy in the last few

weeks and that 99 per cent of the people who were going to fight
to the death for the principle had not the faintest notion what
they were talking about.'[19]

In the early spring of 1918 Redmond returned to London a
broken man; he had been seriously ill for several months, and in
early March he entered hospital for an operation to remove an
internal obstruction. The operation was successfully carried out,
but on 6 March he died suddenly as a result of heart failure.
Perhaps mercifully, he did not live to see the Convention's final
report embodying a very incomplete measure of agreement for
the government's decision to apply conscription to Ireland.

Redmond had been in poor health for some time, but his
death came as a surprise. Reactions were mixed. When his
remains reached Kingstown (now Dún Laoghaire) for burial (in
Wexford), no priest of the diocese of Dublin met the coffin—'so
intense was the bitterness against his policy . . . Great honour,
however, was done it at Westminster Cathedral, and in his native
town.'[20] A few weeks before his death the sympathetic *Daily
Chronicle* had declared: 'One of the things implanted in [national-
ist Ireland's] deeper consciousness is reverent appreciation of Mr
Redmond. The nobly unselfish, devoted career, without spot or
stain, the high note of chivalry and loyalty . . . all this is graven
deep in the Irish people.' The *Northern Whig* in Belfast was
unimpressed: 'Mr Redmond is no Irish "saviour of society". He is
only an incident in Irish politics.'[21] This latter, less flattering
verdict, had all the force of political realism behind it.

'Redmondism', however, was to have one more victory to
savour. His son, Captain William Archer Redmond, rushed to
Waterford and found that here, at least, the Redmond name
could still carry the day. A short pamphlet was published which
stressed the late leader's good works for the city: 'It shows how he
obtained money for the erection of the Waterford free bridge,
now a standing monument to his name and that before and since
the beginning of the war, Mr Redmond secured thousands of
pounds for the housing of the working classes and that he was
able to secure the establishment of the National Cartridge
Factory, which employs hundreds of hands and pays hundreds of
pounds weekly in wages to the workers.'[22] 'Labour must not wait,'
declared Captain Redmond—in a direct thrust against the

attitude of de Valera and Sinn Féin. The Redmondite leaflet insisted: 'To Mr Redmond alone was due the taking over of Irish railways by the government and the subsequent increases of wages which all sections of Irish railway workers are now receiving.' On the historic hill of Ballybricken, in particular, it was declared that every house is 'Redmondite to the backbone'. Captain Redmond easily defeated his Sinn Féin opponent, Dr Vincent J. White, by 1,242 votes to 745; perhaps even more remarkably, he repeated the victory during the Sinn Féin landslide in the 1918 general election.

CONCLUSION

'He was the centre of some important social mechanism, and something was forever expected of him, which he must perform or people would be grieved and disappointed; but if he did this and that, all would be well; and he did whatever was required of him, but still the happy result remained in the future.'[1] This is Tolstoy's celebrated description of the rather passive Count Pierre Bezuhov in *War and Peace*; it is tempting to see John Redmond in the same light.

Conor O'Kelly, the Mayo Nationalist M.P., did indeed see Redmond in precisely that light:

> The leaders of Mr Redmond have taken his measure to the inch, they know their man. They know that he will sacrifice anything to retain his 'leadership'. He abandoned the land conference to do it. He abandoned William O'Brien to do it. He abandoned Tim Healy to do it. In fact there is nothing he is not willing to abandon to save that particular piece of furniture he uneasily sits in. In a word, if Mr Redmond wishes to sit in the chair, he must always be content to be sat upon. That is the price exacted. He pays up and looks as pleasant as he can.[2]

The implication is clear: Redmond had a conciliatory agenda, 'a plea for concord between the two races that Providence has designed should work as neighbours together'—as he put it in his last words in parliament. But this agenda remained hidden as the chairman of the party was forced to pursue the twin objectives of survival and party unity. As Warre B. Wells explained, 'In retrospect, one sees the dominant purpose of his political life emerging from his career as a recurrent *motif* of gathering force: the Recess Committee, the Land Conference, the Convention, that last chance of recovering the lost and misused opportunity which the war created—in these episodes most unmistakably the purpose grows and broadens.'[3] But this was indeed 'in retrospect'; often at the moment of any given crisis Redmond's public meaning was deliberately ambiguous and unclear.

Yet Conor O'Kelly's assessment, while containing indisputable elements of truth, would not be a balanced one. All those who within nationalism offered Redmond different and potentially more fruitful courses behaved like *prima donnas*; Tim Healy and William O'Brien—and it was O'Brien who above all had the thoughtful ideas—flounced on and off stage when it suited them. The effect was to increase the leverage of the less imaginative John Dillon and later Joe Devlin with his Ancient Order of Hibernians machine. The Unionists—in particular, the Ulster Unionists—were even less helpful. It is exasperating to read the later quite genuine expressions of goodwill towards John (or Willie) Redmond which emanated from senior Unionists and contrast them with the rather more tart exchanges before the summer of 1914.[4] As for the radical nationalist critique, Stephen Gwynn has given the best possible reply:

> When that critical hour came, Redmond knew in his bones the weight of Ireland's history; he knew all the propensities which would instantly tend to assert themselves unless their play was checked by a strong counter-emotion . . . Everything depended on an instant and almost desperate move. He might have left the sole offer of service from Ireland to lie with Sir Edward Carson. What he did actually was to offer instantly all that the Ulsterman had offered, and more, for he proposed active union in Ireland itself. It was a bold stroke, but it was guided by an ideal perpetually present with him— the essential unity of Ireland. To set Irishmen working together at such a crisis in the common name of Ireland was an object for which he was willing to jeopardise the whole organisation which stood behind him, at a moment when he spoke of full right for three-fourths of his countrymen.[5]

Redmond's great weaknesses remain—particularly on the Ulster question. He had declared at Wexford in 1888: 'If Home Rule were to mean Rome Rule, he for one would not be a Home Ruler';[6] but confronted by the McCann affair he had lapsed into silence. On the sensitive Ulster issues, he appeared to be under the control of Joe Devlin: 'he must toe the line as Devlin directs'.[7] There is a view that Redmond was 'let down by everyone', in particular the Ulster Unionists, British Tories, and both the War Office and the British government—most notably by Lloyd George during the war. But this is to ignore the convictions of the Ulster Unionists,[8] the relative indeterminacy of view among British Tories[9] on the eve of the Home Rule crisis, and the priorities of the British war machine locked in a life-or-death struggle with imperial Germany.[10]

As a useful corrective to the view of a politician 'let down by everyone',[11] Michael MacDonagh has left us a picture of Redmond at his zenith: 'Anyone who met Redmond early in the year 1916, in the private room he had at the House of Commons as leader of a party, might have heard him, as he smoked his cigar, indulging in happy anticipations respecting the Nationalist cause.'[12]   Redmond, at this moment, had been successful in preventing conscription for Ireland, while at the same time his support for the British war effort had allowed much warmer relationships to form with erstwhile opponents such as Bonar Law and Carson. It is not surprising that he could see no cloud in the sky. Nor is it surprising that Redmond himself tended to place the blame for the collapse of his strategy on those radical nationalists who, he believed, never really understood it in the first place.

Yet it was the radical nationalists who won and imposed their vision on an independent Ireland. It is easy enough to say that the militant speeches of even the moderate Redmond gave them their licence.[13] In particular, the claim that 'they would rather be governed badly by their own Parliament than well' by the Westminster parliament is more than a rhetorical flourish; it is a vital clue to much of twentieth-century Irish history.

But all of this—pertinent comment though it is—ignores Redmond's place in the balance of forces: his significance as a politician who was trying to make himself a bridge from one dispensation to another. The clues are all there as to Redmond's vision of a self-governing Ireland. Substantial symbolic links between Dublin and London would remain—in particular the link of the crown and the Empire. Irish M.P.s would continue to sit at Westminster, and some would now join cabinets. Economic ties would also be close, and Ireland would continue to benefit from British subvention. Cultural nationalism would have a significant but decidedly limited role. The Irish Party would dissolve, and, with it, the tradition of agrarian radicalism. Erstwhile Unionists would have a disproportionately influential role to play in the new southern state, in particular through the agency of the Senate. Even though the new political entity of

Northern Ireland was to remain outside the operation of the Dublin parliament, it would be governed by a system of direct rule characterised by a noticeably green tinge, while the Council of Ireland arrangement enabled the continuance—in theory at least—of the link with Dublin and, thereby, the all-Ireland dimension. Redmond wanted to move from a position of leader of the nationalist bloc to a position as leader of Ireland; no one else in the twentieth century has come remotely as close to achieving this objective as he did. We should record the scale of the ambition even as we record its failure.

NOTES

Introduction

[1] Stephen Gwynn, *John Redmond's Last Years* (London, 1919), p. 338.

[2] Michael MacDonagh, *The Life of William O'Brien, the Irish Nationalist* (London, 1928), p. 228.

[3] Francis Cruise O'Brien, 'John Redmond', *The Leader*, 29 Feb.1910.

[4] Ibid.

[5] *Irish Times*, 1 Mar. 1973.

[6] Ibid., 26 Mar. 1996.

[7] Ibid., 22 Apr. 1996.

1

[1] *Weekly Freeman's Journal* (hereafter *W.F.J.*), 9 Mar. 1918.

[2] Terence Denman, *A Lonely Grave: The Life and Death of William Redmond* (Dublin, 1995), p. 18. There is also the confusing tale of Father John Redmond, who appears to have been a moderate but was hanged nonetheless by the yeomanry (see Daniel Gahan, *The People's Rising: Wexford 1798* (Dublin, 1995), p. 263).

[3] Warre B. Wells, *John Redmond* (London, 1919), p. 40.

[4] L. G. Redmond-Howard, *John Redmond* (London, 1910), p. 246.

[5] Note Griffith's pique against the U.K. university system provoked by a lecture on that topic by a wealthy Redmondite, J. P. Boland, who had been educated at Christ Church, Oxford (*United Irishman*, 22 Oct. 1904). Griffith was also intensely antisemitic: 'No thoughtful Irishman or Irishwomen can view without apprehension the continuous influx of Jews into Ireland and the continuous efflux of the native population' (*United Irishman*, 9 Jan. 1904). Redmond, on the other hand, spoke out against the Limerick pogrom and later offered a parliamentary seat to a prominent Dublin Jewish solicitor. I owe this point to Dr Patrick Maume.

[6] Denman, *A Lonely Grave*, p. 23.

[7] *W.F.J.*, 9 Mar. 1918.

[8] Doubt has been cast on the accuracy of Gladstone's perception; for example, Parnell's close analysis of the figures did not confirm it (see *United Ireland*, 10 Sept. 1881). For the Tyrone by-election see Frank Wright, *Two Lands on One Soil: Ulster Politics before Home Rule* (Dublin, 1996), p. 472.

[9] Paul Bew, *C. S. Parnell* (Dublin, 1980), p. 55.

[10] 'Wexford Obeying Parnell', from the *Wexford People*, reprinted in *United Ireland*, 12 Nov. 1881; also 3 Dec. 1881. W. E. Vaughan, *Landlords and Tenants in Mid-Victorian Ireland* (Oxford, 1994), pp 283–5, shows Wexford's relative quiescence.

[11] Wells, *Redmond*, pp 40–41 William O'Brien saw Redmond, even at this heady moment, as a man 'little inclined to headstrong passion' (*Recollections* (London, 1905), p. 352). As early as April 1882 government circles regarded Redmond as 'moderate' and 'decent' (*Florence Arnold-Forster's Irish Journal*, ed. T. W. Moody and Richard Hawkins, with Margaret Moody (Oxford, 1988), p. 458 (entry for 26 Apr. 1882)).

[12] Denman, *A Lonely Grave*, p. 27; Patrick O'Farrell, *The Irish in Australia* (Sydney, 1986), pp 225–7.

[13] *The Speaker's Handbook on the Irish Question, by an Irish Liberal* (London, n.d.), p. 45.

[14] *W.F.J.*, 21 July 1883.

[15] Ibid.

[16] Denis Gwynn, *The Life of John Redmond* (London, 1932), p. 55.

[17] *Speaker's Handbook*, p. 49.

[18] *Daily News*, 20 July 1888.

[19] *Enniscorthy Guardian*, 11 Dec. 1886.

[20] *W.F.J.*, 9 Mar. 1918. For a sceptical view of Redmond's agrarian activities in this period see W. H. Hurlbert, *Ireland under Coercion: The Diary of an American* (Edinburgh, 1889), p. 194.

[21] H. C. G. Matthew (ed.), *The Gladstone Diaries, 1887–1891*, vol. xii (Oxford, 1994), p. 256. This meeting on 18–19 December 1889 was the second such meeting; after the first (8 March 1888) Gladstone wrote of Parnell: 'Undoubtedly his tone was very conservative.' After the second meeting in 1889 he added: 'He is certainly one of the best people to deal with that I have ever known.' Gladstone's 'secret' note adds: 'I may say, however, that we were quite agreed in thinking the real difficulty lies in determining the particular form in which an Irish representation may have to be retained at Westminster. We conversed at large on different modes. He has no absolute or forgone conclusion.' Later, in the throes of the divorce crisis, Parnell alleged that these discussions had been highly unsatisfactory from a nationalist point of view; it is not a view which finds any support in the *Gladstone Diaries* or indeed in Parnell's public or private references before the divorce crisis broke. (See also Edward Byrne, 'Parnellism', *Irish Weekly Independent*, 8 Oct. 1896.) Redmond, though, fully accepted Parnell's version as against Gladstone's (*The Parnellite Split or the Disruption of the Irish Parliamentary Party*, from *The Times*, with an introduction (London, 1891), p. 55.

[22] *United Ireland*, 21 Dec. 1889.

[23] D. Gwynn, *Life of Redmond*, p. 53.

[24] Ibid., p. 297.

[25] *W.F.J.*, 9 Mar.1918.

[26] *The Parnellite Split*, p. 179.

[27] *The Leader*, 26 Feb. 1910.

[28] Lord George Hamilton, *Parliamentary Reminiscences and Reflections, 1868–1885* (London, 1906), p. 222.

[29] A. M. Sullivan, *Old Ireland* (London, 1917), p. 48.

[30] Wells, *Redmond*, p. 25.

[31] Sullivan, *Old Ireland*, p. 48.

[32] See Frank Callanan, *The Parnell Split, 1890–91* (Cork, 1992), pp 276–307.

[33] T. P. O'Connor, *Memoirs of an Old Parliamentarian* (2 vols, London, 1929), i, 331.

[34] *Irish Times*, 1 Mar. 1973.

[35] The language of Redmond's will—in which he gave priority to his bequest of his guns and horses to his son—is a testimony to his love of country sports.

2

[1] Charles Stewart Parnell Hamilton, *East, West: An Irish Doctor's Memoirs* (London, 1955), p. 18. Redmond was to become close to this family—who were not relations.

[2] D. Gwynn, *Life of Redmond*, pp 86–7.

[3] *Irish Weekly Independent*, 8 Feb. 1896.

[4] Redmond-Howard, *Redmond*, p. 87.

[5] D. Gwynn, *Life of Redmond*, p. 88.

[6] Maev Sullivan, *No Man's Man* (Dublin, 1943), pp 294–5; see also T. D. Sullivan, *Recollections of Troubled Times in Irish Politics* (Dublin, 1905), p. 341.

[7] 'Home Rule: what has become of it?', reprinted in *Irish Weekly Independent*, 8 Nov. 1894.

[8] Redmond to Mather, 28 Apr. 1892 (NLI, MS 15206).

[9] *Black and White*, quoted in *Irish Weekly Independent*, 5 Aug. 1893.

[10] *Northern Whig*, 23 May 1891.

[11] Thomas Andrews is the subject of sharp criticism in Denis Gwynn's *Life of John Redmond*, p. 205. Andrews had said in a *Morning Post* statement of 19 December 1910 that 'If we are deserted by Great Britain, I would rather be governed by Germany than by Patrick Ford and John Redmond and company.' This is a doubly revealing incident. Andrews had worked in a broadminded way alongside Redmond on the Recess Committee (see Sir Horace Plunkett's praise on this point in his letter to Andrews of 19 April 1912, reprinted in Shan F. Bullock, *Thomas Andrews: Shipbuilder* (with an introduction by Sir Horace Plunkett) (Dublin & London, 1912), p. 79. Andrews, in the heat of the Home Rule crisis, seems to have forgotten the experience, but it also seems that the historian Gwynn was unaware of the previous connection. The Recess Committee involved Redmond in certain political risks. At one point in 1895 he signed a joint statement which declared that the Irish farmer's methods were the 'most simple and barbarous in Western Europe'; words like these stung, and a quarter of a century later Redmond was still being upbraided for this 'unpatriotic' observation (*Nationality*, 4 Apr. 1917).

[12] Paul Bew, *Conflict and Conciliation in Ireland, 1890–1910: Parnellites and Radical Agrarians* (Oxford, 1987), pp 26–34.

[13] Ibid., p. 33.

[14] *The Parnellite*, 18 Feb. 1895.

[15] Wells, *Redmond*, p. 62. As far as James Connolly was concerned, Redmond's record had by 1898 marked him as a right-wing 'reactionist' of an extreme sort (*Forward*, 18 Mar. 1911).

3

[1] Sullivan, *Old Ireland*, p. 136.

[2] *New York Times*, 4 Feb. 1900.

[3] For all these issues see Bew, *Conflict and Conciliation*, chs 3–5.

[4] *United Irishman*, 24 Sept. 1904.

[5] Redmond to Walsh, 7 Apr. 1915 (J. C. Walsh papers, New York Public Library, Box 2, folder 5). I owe this reference to the kindness of Dr Brian S. Murphy.

[6] *The Times*, 13 Apr. 1905.

[7] Sir Robert Anderson, *Sidelights on the Home Rule Movement* (London, 1906), p. 202.

[8] D. D. Sheehan, *Ireland since Parnell* (London, 1921), p. 161.

[9] See Bew, *Conflict and Conciliation*, p. 149.

[10] Ibid., pp 207–8.

[11] *Longford Leader*, 21 Sept. 1907.

[12] *Irish People*, 28 Oct.1907.

[13] J. J. Clancy, *The Irish Party and the Budget: A Vindication* (Dublin, 1910), pp 3–9 ('Why the Irish Party Voted for the Budget', a speech delivered on the second reading of the Finance Bill on 25 April 1910).

[14] Andrew Dunlop, *Fifty Years of Irish Journalism* (Dublin, 1911), p. 292.

[15] Cambridge University Library, Ulster Unionist Council leaflets, series UC69.

[16] *Irish People*, 26 May 1908.

[17] *W.F.J.*, 5 Oct. 1910.

4

[1] 'Irish Protestants and Home Rule', a lecture delivered at the Rotunda, Dublin, 29 Nov. 1886, in *Home Rule Speeches of John Redmond, M.P.* (London, 1910), pp 27–8.

[2] *The Leader*, 13 May 1911.

[3] *W.F.J.*, 23 Nov. 1912.

[4] Ibid., 20 Dec. 1912.

[5] Patricia Jalland, *The Liberals and Ireland* (Brighton, 1980), *passim*.

[6] Bentley Brinkerhoff Gilbert, *David Lloyd George: A Political Life: Organiser of Victory, 1912–16* (London, 1992), p. 94. On 6 February 1912 Lloyd George failed to convince the cabinet of the case for some form of Ulster exclusion. His biographer Professor Gilbert writes: 'Nonetheless, one can say that the failure to adopt at this time Lloyd George's motion for some form of Ulster exclusion constituted one of the most disastrous mistakes of modern British, not to mention Irish, history . . . This needs to be stressed. For one moment, in the spring of 1912 . . . three-quarters of a century of Irish civil war might have been avoided. "If Ulster, or rather any county, had a right to remain outside the Irish Parliament," Bonar Law told Riddell less than a month later, "for my part my objectives would be met." . . . These were the possibilities in the spring of 1912. The chance, once lost, never came again.'

[7] John Redmond, *The Home Rule Bill* (London, 1912), p. 80 (speech at the National Convention, Mansion House, Dublin, 23 Apr. 1912).

[8] Ibid., p. 65 (Redmond's speech on the second reading, 9 May 1912.)

[9] Ibid., p. 85.

[10] *The Leader*, 1 Mar. 1913.

[11] On this topic see Paul Bew, *Ideology and the Irish Question* (Oxford, 1994), pp 84–90.

[12] S. Gwynn, *Last Years*, p. 103. The current leader of the Ulster Unionist Party, David Trimble, seems to agree in substance with Stephen Gwynn's analysis: 'If [Redmond] had made a clear offer of four counties in 1913, would there have been a U.V.F.? Would it have fought alone for Fermanagh and Tyrone?' At the same time, it is worth remembering Lord Milner's advice to Carson, and the reasons for it: 'I hope you stick out for six counties as a minimum. It is really too monstrous that they should make a row about leaving some of their people under the imperial parliament, when we are asked to leave an even greater number of ours in the rest of Ireland under a brand new government in Dublin' (Milner to Carson, 21 July 1914 (PRONI, D1507/A/6/40)). On Devlin's popularity and ability to put pressure on Redmond see Lovat Fraser's *Tour of Ireland in 1913*, ed. Jane Marsland (Belfast, 1992), p. 18.

[13] *W.F.J.*, 9 Mar. 1918.

[14] On this point see James Comyn's memoir of Carson in *Justice of the Peace*, 6 Nov. 1993. I owe this reference to George Woodman.

[15] Sir Dunbar Plunkett Barton, *Tim Healy: Memories and Anecdotes* (Dublin, n.d.), pp 83–91.

[16] Gilbert, *Lloyd George*, pp 103–4. Interestingly, though, Stephen Gwynn never seems to have been told of this.

[17] MacDonagh, *William O'Brien*, p. 198. This is a convincing explicit challenge to Stephen Gwynn's interpretation in *Last Years*.

[18] Bew, *Ideology and the Irish Question*, p. 120.

5

[1] S. Gwynn, *Last Years*, p. 222.

[2] Ibid., p. 224.

[3] Sullivan, *Old Ireland*, p. 202.

[4] S. Gwynn, *Last Years*, p. 224.

[5] Ibid., p. 239.

[6] Ibid. For Lloyd George's difficulties and Carson's genuine attempts at compromise see Gilbert, *Llord George*, pp 322–34.

[7] *W.F.J.*, 26 May 1917.

[8] Ibid.

[9] Ibid.

[10] Ibid.

[11] Ibid.

[12] This account is based on S. Gwynn, *Last Years.*

[13] *W.F.J.*, 20 Oct. 1917; T. M. Healy, *Letters and Leaders of My Day* (2 vols, London, 1928), ii, 587.

[14] *W.F.J.*, 27 Oct. 1917.

[15] *Irish Times*, 1 Mar. 1973. This crowd apparently included C. S. 'Todd' Andrews, later to be a Fianna Fáil *apparatchik* of some note; it is tempting to see this moment as a symbol of the handover of power from the old 'nomenclatura' to the new.

[16] *Weekly Northern Whig*, 19 Jan. 1918.

[17] *W.F.J.*, 26 Jan. 1918.

[18] Ibid.

[19] Plunkett Foundation, Oxford, Plunkett Papers, ADA 36, 2 Mar. 1918. I owe this reference to Dr Patrick Maume.

[20] Healy, *Letters and Leaders,* ii, 592.

[21] *Weekly Northern Whig*, 2 Feb. 1918.

[22] *W.F.J.*, 23 Mar. 1918.

Conclusion

[1] Leo Tolstoy, *War and Peace* (Penguin Classic ed.), p. 233.

[2] This letter was placed in the *Irish Times*, 27 July 1993, by the family of the late Conor O'Kelly M.P.

[3] Wells, *Redmond*, p. 204.

[4] See Bew, *Ideology and the Irish Question*, p. 141.

[5] S. Gwynn, *Last Years*, pp 339–40.

[6] Laurence M. Geary, *The Plan of Campaign, 1886–1891* (Cork, 1986), p. 87.

[7] Lovat Fraser, senior *Times* correspondent, to Geoffrey Robinson, Editor of *The Times*, 12, 13 Oct. 1913, printed in *Lovat Fraser's Tour of Ireland in 1913*, ed. Jane Marsland (Belfast, 1992), p. 18.

[8] Stephen Gwynn's *D.N.B.* entry pays a full tribute to Redmond's ability to reassure English opinion. He adds however: 'But the real difficulty which Redmond had to face lay in Ulster, of which, like most Irishmen of the South, he knew little.'

[9] This diary comment (7 Nov. 1910) of a senior Tory is worth noting: 'The Ulster members are firing blank cartridges about devolution, banging the Orange drum, and denouncing in future those of us who may concede something to Nationalism. In point of fact, these friends of ours do not occupy the secure foothold they held ten or twenty years ago. England is bored about Home Rule,

but in view of recent legislation less hostile than ever. The passage of the R.C. University Bill and the Accession Declaration Bill show that the Orange mob is less sensitive than before, and William O'Brien is a fitful guarantee that the northern spirit will not be without sympathy in the South. All these symptoms tend to reconcile England to home rule. Moreover, one of these days we shall wake to find that Labour has swept Belfast, while liberalism may yet again find a place in rural Ulster' (*The Crawford Papers: The Journal of David Lindsay, Twenty-Seventh Earl of Crawford and Tenth Earl of Balcarres, 1871–1940, during the years 1892–1940*, ed. John Vincent (Manchester, 1984), p. 166. Yet Balcarres was to function as a loyal and effective supporter of Bonar Law during the Home Rule crisis—in part because of a dismissive attitude towards Redmond: 'Redmond is becoming turgid. With his growing stomach, he has lost all that incisive analysis which ten years ago marked his speeches' (ibid., p. 99). This is the diary entry for 21 Dec. 1906 and evokes the concern of many Tories that Redmond had been unable to sustain the conciliatory tone of the mid-1890s.

[10] On the issue of the military establishment's insensitivity to nationalist sentiment, see the modulated comments in D. G. Boyce, *The Sure Confusing Drum: Ireland and the First World War* (Swansea, 1993), p. 20; Terence Denman, *Ireland's Unknown Soldiers* (Dublin, 1992). It also ignores the strong feeling expressed by, for example, the London correspondent of the *Northern Whig*, that Redmond abandoned conciliation once he obtained the balance of power (*Weekly Northern Whig*, 9 Mar. 1918).

[11] This is Terence de Vere White's view in 'The Tragedy of John Redmond', *Irish Times*, 1 Mar. 1973.

[12] MacDonagh, *William O'Brien*, p. 205. Redmond wrote the introduction for MacDonagh's *The Irish at the Front* (London, 1916) and expressed his supreme confidence that the 'young men of Ireland' were warm supporters of his policy (p. 13).

[13] Frank Hugh O'Donnell was particularly upset by Redmond's affectionate public reference in 1908 to the Irish-American extremist Patrick Ford (*A History of the Irish Parliamentary Party* (2 vols, London, 1910), ii, 195), while others might point to Redmond's ambiguous private conversation with Roger Casement on 7 May 1914: Redmond's parting words to Casement were: 'Well, Sir Roger, I don't mind you getting an Irish republic if you can' (B. L. Reid, *The Lives of Sir Roger Casement* (New Haven & London, 1976), p. 191).

SELECT BIBLIOGRAPHY

During his life Redmond was the subject of a biography, *John Redmond*, published by L. G. Redmond-Howard, a kinsman, in London, 1910. Following his death, there were two interesting studies which were rapidly published: Warre B. Wells, *John Redmond* (London) and Stephen Gwynn, *John Redmond's Last Years* (London); both appeared in 1919. Both are valuable, but Gwynn's book is outstanding, though it does, for the earlier period of Redmond's life, need to be supplemented by Stephen Gwynn's *Dictionary of National Biography* entry for Redmond, which also contains valuable material based on his personal knowledge of the Irish leader. In 1932, basing his account largely on the Redmond Papers in the National Library of Ireland, Denis Gwynn published his lengthy and immensely valuable *The Life of John Redmond* (London); although it is weak on agrarian matters—in particular, the ranch war—Gwynn is generally sound on Redmond's career as such. But when it comes to the broader canvas, there are a number of slips which reveal a less than sound grasp of British or Ulster Unionist politics: party labels and designations of office are misplaced, and the Orange Order is confused with a more narrowly based splinter-group, as is the Presbyterian Church. The combined effect of such slips is to exaggerate the level of bigotry present in Unionist politics; complex issues are at times simplified and moralised away. The *Irish Times* has recently published two important essays on Redmond and Redmondism: Patrick Maume, 'The Tragedy of John Redmond—Visionary Statesman or Traitor?', 4 Mar. 1993; and Kevin Myers, 'A Great Reconciler Is Traduced Again', 23 Apr. 1996. Another recent discussion is Robert C. Redmond, 'Ireland's Forgotten Patriot' in the *Contemporary Review,* July 1994. Redmond was rather surprisingly omitted from *The Blackwell Biographical Dictionary of British Political Life in the Twentieth Century* (Oxford, 1990), but will be the subject of a new treatment (as will be Parnell) in the new *Dictionary of National Biography* being prepared under the editorship of Professor H. C. G. Matthew. Michael Laffan, 'John Redmond (1856–1918) and Home Rule', an essay in Ciaran Brady (ed.), *Worsted in the Game: Losers in Irish History* (Dublin, 1989), is an interesting published version of a Thomas Davis Lecture first broadcast in 1987.

Two most useful volumes of Redmond's speeches are *Home Rule: Speeches of John Redmond, M.P.*, edited with an introduction by R. Barry O'Brien (London, 1910) and *The Home Rule Bill* (London, 1912).   There is certain amount of context for Redmond's career to be found in Paul Bew, *Land and the National Question in Ireland, 1858–82* (Dublin, 1978); *C. S. Parnell* (Dublin, 1980); *Conflict and Conciliation in Ireland, 1890–1910* (Oxford, 1987); and *Ideology and the Irish Question* (Oxford, 1994). Thomas P. Dooley, *Irishmen or English Soldiers?* (Liverpool, 1995) sheds much new and fascinating light on Redmondism and Waterford politics and Redmond's role as a local representative.